SPEECH MAKERS BIBLE

Write and deliver
speeches that hit the mark

Kevin Balshaw

National Library of Australia
Cataloguing-in-Production entry:

Balshaw, Kevin
Speech makers bible.

1st ed.

ISBN 978 0 646 49127 1

Speechwriting. Public speaking.

808.51

Published by Q2write.com
with CreateSpace, an Amazon.com company

To the world's messengers,
many of them posthumously.

Contents

Preface

The genesis for this book goes back to my early teenage years in the far west of Victoria on the southern corner of Australia when a teacher/mentor at the rough and tumble Casterton High School, a country version of Collingwood Grammar as I regarded it, persuaded me to give up my nights by a kerosene lamp with soft-cover westerns and detective stories and begin a lifetime's interest in the pages of history's finest literature.

It was not long before I was committed to a path in life far outside the mould of the times and the place of my upbringing, where in general the options were to work on a farm, shear sheep, repair cars, join the council road gang leaning on their shovels or, at the higher end of life's aspirations, balance the day's takings in the local bank. Reading set off a creative itch that I came to realise had been inherently vested in me. I would write—and have done ever since.

An amateur and amateurish period of writing through my school years—the gospels phase—accounted for the fact that English was the only subject I passed in the final year. After that and a brief itinerant existence, mostly writing poetry in coffee shops in Melbourne and Adelaide, I secured a cadetship in journalism at the Hamilton Spectator, back in my home territory. The experience through my early years there was a blunt and unforgiving initiation from which I have to thank a number of gifted mentors, mainly latter day itinerants on the country news circuit, for teaching me to write tight news copy and translate that style into more creative feature writing. It also led to my elevation at age 23 to the position of editor.

I worked more than twenty years in the media—a mix of print, radio and television—before reaching what might be termed revelations, a change of direction into feeding and managing the media, managing web sites and speechwriting for politicians. For this transition that began one of the most interesting, challenging and pressure-charged times in my life, I have to thank Tom Wallace, former conservative National Party member for Gippsland South in the Victorian Parliament. Tom engaged me part-time to write his media releases and speeches. Subsequently Peter McGauran, who went on to be a minister in the Howard Government, used my services, as did the State Upper House member for Gippsland, Peter Hall.

Working for them led in 1990 to an appointment as press secretary and speechwriter to the Victorian National Party leader, Pat McNamara. Through two grinding years in opposition, which I wouldn't wish on anyone although it was probably a good apprenticeship, I came increasingly under the attention of the Nationals' senior coalition partner, the Liberals. As it became clear Victoria's first woman Premier, Joan Kirner, was about to call an election in the spring of 1992, I was drafted to join the Liberals' media team, which made three of us. The story that leader Jeff Kennett and his people plied to the Nationals was that they wanted a cohesive Coalition media unit covering both parties for the campaign. But from that point on, I was firmly entrenched with the Liberal Party.

Kennett came to me halfway through the campaign and said, 'Pat is going to offer you a job in government as a tourism adviser, but the offer is open if you want to be one of my press secretaries. Give me an answer by tomorrow.' There's no question, I told him on the spot, I'll take it.

Through his seven-year reign as Premier, I was his keynote speechwriter, penned his suggested Preamble to the Australian Constitution during the republic debate, vetted most of the other speeches prepared for him by advisers, and oversaw whole-of-government communications, the transformation to online government and the development and management of government web sites.

I was the anchor for writing the campaign launch speeches for Kennett at elections in 1992, 1996 and 1999, co-ordinated policy development for the 1996 and 1999 elections, wrote speeches for formal openings of the Parliament for Governors Richard McGarvie and Mr Justice Sir James Gobbo, and through the 1999 election project managed the infamous jeff.com.au web site, which for the best part of a decade retained the mantle as the most successful political site in the history of the Net in Australia.

On 19 October 1999, after a month with the result in the balance, Kennett conceded defeat in an election he had been expected to win by a country mile. The carnival was over. From the next day, I was working with a number of corporate clients I had lined up—a free agent writing speeches for company leaders including Wayne Bos, then head of the Sausage dot com group, Dr Ziggy Switkowski and his management team at Telstra, Malcolm Broomhead, first at mining house North Ltd and later at Orica Australia, Marcia Coleman as chairman of the national co-ordinating body for organ and tissue donation, Australians Donate, the peak pharmaceutical industry body, the Australian Davos Connection, for leading figures (who should remain nameless) on both sides of the political fence, and, in a rare excursion into the sporting world, for Alicia Molik's first public appearance following the 2005 Australian Tennis Open.

This combined with corporate affairs, media relations, marketing plans and web site projects for corporates, government departments and non-government organisations.

My life as a free agent continues—a blend of work/lifestyle that depends on my attitude and initiative and ideas and the vicissitudes of the market, of holding to the independence it provides and waking in a cold sweat in the middle of the night in the lean months. Whatever happens next, the devil may care. I am indebted to my elder daughter, Angela, for a saying that has become integral to my philosophy: We'll burn that bridge when we come to it!

From this background, my guide to speechwriting is set in the creative arena of contemporary Australia, with ample historical references to back it, and derives from a lifetime devoted to writing, and writing the spoken word.

Kevin Balshaw

1. The world's a stage

Speechwriting has an air of mystery about it—the kind of thing someone else does, but you don't quite know how, or how they can make it fit together so that the end result is coherent, effective and almost seem like it might have been easy. Even more daunting can be the combined task of writing and delivering your own speech. For most people, public speaking is one of their greatest fears, out on the edge of unknowing like a first-time parachutist.

But if you've sat through a speech that worked well and seemed like it was easy, as if it was a wordsmith's gem and the speaker made it sound like it was second nature to them, that is precisely the destination we're going to arrive at. Dispel the fears, set out a practical, step-by-step guide that makes it straightforward and easy, and give you the confidence to write and, if you're the one in the frontline, deliver a good speech that will have people talking about it and what an engaging public performer you are.

I have been doing this for a quarter century. I must admit trepidation still surfaces at the outset when a speech assignment comes in. But that ends immediately the task is assessed and there is an appreciation of what lies ahead, the deadlines and how it is to be handled. Then the excitement of the chase—the challenge—takes over. It becomes a matter of setting out on a new adventure, often pioneering unknown territory, gaining a commanding knowledge in fields that may never have been contemplated. And by applying a sequential, planned approach, it builds with surety towards an end result you can be confident will work, and work well.

If it is the case that stratospheric anxiety levels are your initial reaction, be comforted that you are not on your own. Aside from a lifetime's writing and my specific experience at handling speeches, I continue to be sought out as a speechwriter to company executives and the like for two basic reasons. The lesser is that the internal corporate affairs units are generally preoccupied with the day's immediate priorities—either in defensive or crisis mode trying to get their organisation out of a deep hole that a media report or political comment has put it in, and it will be exactly the same tomorrow and the day after and ... It's much like the concept of the paperless office, an idea filled with good intentions, and that is as far as it goes. The main thing, though, is the sheer terror that strikes in the ranks of corporate affairs when the chief strides from his office, six-shooters strapped on, saying he has accepted a keynote speech engagement and he wants it to be a humdinger. You see, it happens even at high level in the professional environment. The easiest solution for them is to say we have an expert out there, hand it on to him. Corporate affairs, along with many other people in the organisation, become the experts only when the draft is in and they can pick it to pieces and seek to put their territorial mark on it.

As the Beatles put it, for people right across the scale there will be an answer. Just let it be.

Convince yourself first

BASICALLY, WE NEED to be convinced and convincing—to ourselves and others. There is a need to build confidence, not only for the writer but the person who is to deliver the speech, sometimes one and the same person. Beware that in the absence of thorough, methodical planning you run a real risk of getting lost in a maze of stumbling rhetoric and end up unable to present a convincing case and relate a compelling story.

In the course of this exercise, we will show you how to resolve the range of issues that are common to speechwriting. One is a lack of access to a busy executive, which means often the writer has to work in isolation from the speaker. There is a need to get to know them in other ways and second guess them in the context of their speaking engagement. Conflicting currents often emerge within an organisation over what the speech should say, what it should not say. Suddenly everyone is an expert speechwriter. The real writer needs to take ownership and not let it get lost and diffused in an internal committee process—and often that takes a measure of raw courage. These internal processes will be pushing for the speech to echo the corporate mantras and brand themes, use catch-terms and euphemisms and convey the message in language that either saps it of meaning or veils the real intent, all of which should be resisted. Most important for the quality of the end result is that the writer is able to exercise a mastery of the language, looking critically and analytically at the written word on the page and being able to perceive how it will resonate in the delivery—the written spoken word.

The issues I have set out always have to be taken into account, but they are by no means insurmountable barriers. These are the peripherals we deal with: the speech is the big picture and we stick with it.

Writing speeches relies on a range of talents and requires flexibility—an innate deftness in developing imagery and ideas—to fit an intellectual and creative exercise to a specific occasion. To the promise that there will be an answer, there is. It calls for thorough preparation and planning, to know where the traps are set and how not to get caught in them, to follow the plan to its logical conclusion, and throughout to apply the faculties of imagination and creativity that are essential to make it live and capture an audience's attention.

This guide will give everyone who has to utter a word in a formal public situation an insight into the fact that the world's a stage and if they happen to occupy centre stage they can handle it in style.

What you will discover from this guide is a case that argues the importance of speeches in communication, provides an extensive range of examples and case studies and a step-by-step guide to the result you want … without ever having to strap on a parachute:

- The critical role of the speech in the communication function of all kinds of organisations, along with some inspiration that will give you the confidence to develop a speech and, if it is your lot, deliver it;

- Speeches that hit the mark—the elements of a great speech, along with examples of the best and the worst from both earlier and modern times and some notable clangers that will demonstrate what to avoid;

- Speech formats from full text to short-handed dot points, and an evaluation of the use and over-use of Powerpoint slides;

- The importance of establishing the context of the speech;

- Knowing your speaker;

- Knowing your subject, incorporating the most effective research methods;

- Planning the structure of the speech and writing it;

- Case studies and examples—many of them from way out of the normal mould, based on my judgment, and many that derive from my direct experience;

- The process of speech development step by step from assignment to final approval;

- Setting out promotional and media strategies to get maximum value from an address;

- Final assessment—feedback and evaluation to put the writer and presenter in better tune for next time; and

- A guide to achieving the most effective delivery with ease and confidence.

Although I began writing political speeches in the early 1980s, the real origin of my experience on a higher plane dates from 1992 when I started work as the writer in newly-elected Victorian Premier Jeff Kennett's political office. They dubbed me with one of those titles that were commonly used in the medieval royal courts—a lordly title, but one that designates the functionary's place in the scheme of things. Accordingly, take this as a lesson from the scribe of the Court of Kennett (and, before and since then, of many other places and people), dignified as *The Lord of the Quill.*

2. The speech in communications

A speech is the most fundamental means of communication, but defining its form, function and potential impact is more complex than that obvious observation. Every speech has a specifically targeted application, and must be written accordingly. In the narrowest sense, for the particular event or occasion for which it is prepared, the speech imparts a message to a select audience. But it is able to reach a mass audience via broadcast or reproduction in the media. The spoken word is transient, but the text from which it is delivered gives it permanence. It lends itself to becoming an enduring record through publication in the media, on a web site or intranet or by distribution to groups beyond the immediate audience. As evidence of the importance that key public figures and their organisations accord their speeches, note that most political and corporate web sites feature a special page for speeches in addition to their news pages.

It is the intrinsically enduring nature of the speech that gives lie to the self-composed epitaph of the poet John Keats—indeed that is reinforced by the endurance of his work—that, 'Here lies one whose name was writ in water.'

A significant qualification to bear in mind is that the speech is intrinsically different to any other form of writing. One of the things that makes it different, and the reason anxiety levels build up in speechwriters and speakers alike, is that the speech is a performance piece. Speeches are capable of making an impact above the scope of any other form of communication in that they are interactive experiences between the speaker and their audience, and that largely they are delivered to a group of people who are there out of a common interest. That interest, it should be mentioned, could be friendly or hostile, or a mix of both. Nevertheless, the people in the audience have made a special effort to be there. They want to get the message, and that in itself should help engender confidence. A direct, personal relationship establishes between an individual at the centre of attention and an entity, the audience, that is present to capture not only a message but something of the character, beliefs and ideas of the person presenting it.

The performance of the speaker—and the calibre of the text they work from—goes a long way to building a responsive atmosphere and countering hostility. It can breach new frontiers; it can inspire and uplift; it can offer leadership that gives people courage to embark into the unknown; it can instruct and inform; like a great piece of music, a book or movie, it can create expectation and it can move people to tears. At the other end of the scale, it can bore them to tears.

Speeches offer distinct advantages as a communication mode in the modern era. While people will devote time to attend and take in a speech, many of the other forms of communication we use end up being binned or deleted with a keystroke—as unrecyclable by-products of a lifestyle overcrowded with information and short on time. That places the advantage squarely in the court of the speech.

From observation, only a small proportion of people working in the communication field will have had much experience at speechwriting, but I would emphasise the importance of them broadening their horizons into this area. There is an ironclad case for that contention: the speech is the centrepoint of communication, and a form of communication critical to your organisation and the people who lead it. Therefore, become familiar in the practice to the point at which you are comfortable with it, and likewise for people who might be putting together their own speeches or presentations.

I also re-affirm the point in this context that corporate affairs professionals tend to be so bogged down in the day-to-day communication task of their organisation that they lack the time to research and write a speech and follow it through to final approval. That means it is time for a re-think of the priorities and the way the organisation functions. Accepting speeches as integral to the communication function, the corporate ethos needs to foster the art of speechwriting and give people time to perform the task to a high professional standard. If it is secondary, why bother in the first place? Why not let the CEO, as they are too often prone to do, keep making fools of themselves because they walk unscripted into the public arena and unprepared for the attention that lies in wait for them?

The communications centrepiece

A SPEECH CAN FORM THE CENTREPIECE, or at least a key element, of a broader communications program in the way it helps position an organisation, promotes a particular sector and gets a view across. The potential to create impact and get results elevates the speech to the point where it can become the linchpin around which a communications program is set into effect. It can provide the launch pad for information or marketing campaigns or an ongoing media relations program. It provides the most credible of forums for a position to be explained. It is a key tool in issues management—to build and cement working relations and trust with interest groups and help address their concerns on particular issues. It can herald innovations and initiatives. It provides an essential avenue to position and differentiate an organisation. It is a resource of information of value both internally and externally as to what an organisation stands for and the direction it is taking. A speech of note from an organisation's leader is far more effective, and far more likely to be remembered, than the corporate mission and vision statements. People are able to derive from it an insight into the thinking that propels an organisation and its substance.

It could be argued sitting and listening to a speech is passive. There is always the option of using it as the opportunity for a refreshing nap. But people in the audience have to make the effort in the first place. Furthermore, they are there out of interest and that presents a real opportunity to engage them and get a message across to them in a very personal sense. That goes for all speeches, from the visionary to more instructive or technical presentations.

What has been said in a particular delivery may well come into contention. But in the first place, by its very nature the delivery places the speaker and the organisation they represent in a commanding position to relate their story on their terms. Should it foster wider debate, no matter how hostile, that too serves a positive purpose in drawing attention to it. There is nothing like controversy to inspire a headline and give the talkjocks something to pontificate about.

Confronting great expectations

FEW PEOPLE APPROACH THE PREPARATION of a speech with any sense of ease. Add the dual imposition of having to deliver it, and for most this poses a challenge of the magnitude that triggers a flight response. Let me put this in terms of a workplace situation. Even the pre-knowledge that someone is required to deliver a short address or presentation to a small group of work associates often brings on severe anxiety and anticipation. The same people who recount their weekends comfortably among each other over morning coffee are ill at ease in a formal setting in which suddenly they are made the centre of attention. The perception is that judgment day has arrived and they are in the witness box, their fate hanging on the way they handle themselves and the substantiveness of what they say.

Even for the experienced, the commissioning of a speech usually stirs the kind of doubts that beset one heading into the unknown. We start with a blank page, little more than an outline of the event or an early program, sometimes a designated title, possibly a couple of suggested themes that may be unrelated to the title, and a day sometime too soon for delivery. The originator of the commission may have counted back from delivery, allowing time to absorb internal comments in an interminable succession of drafts and for final approval, and have arrived at a deadline—

invariably a Sunday too near for comfort. And it will beat disquietly with the undertone of big expectations. It comes to the best of us.

What people need to overcome is the fear or expectation of the unknown, as this case will illustrate. I've been at gatherings where maybe just 10 to 15 people come together for a training or thinktank session and are invited at the outset to introduce themselves, describe their positions and explain why they are there and what they want to get out of the program or contribute to it. The majority are clearly dampened by self-consciousness, and it shows. Then there may be one or two who have their heads together. They exude presence. They are succinct. Their natural warmth shines. Everyone else wishes from the depth of their embarrassment, if only I could be like that.

The answer, of course, is that you can. Look upon the speech as a story that builds through a series of critical points to a conclusion. Recall the stories that have held your attention and learn their lessons. You will be relating your story. People want to hear it, to get your take on something that could well be familiar to them but from a different perspective.

It is also helpful to reflect on the experience of meeting a room of people for the first time. As you are introduced around, you will take one of two approaches. You can be overcome by self-consciousness, introspectively thinking only of your own reaction and how you will be perceived. Or you can be the engaging person who projects yourself to them one at a time, forgetting yourself and exercising the interest to get to know them. You will emerge from the self-conscious approach recalling no more than two or three first names and nothing of the people behind the names because you've been focused inwardly; from the second, remembering and knowing most of them, having been prepared in your attitude. The successful preparation and delivery of a speech is much the same. A structured, thought-out approach will create confidence in the preparation of your speech. You can be confident it will relate to the audience, not as a mass but a group of individuals who deserve your respect and interest, and moreover are keenly interested in what you have to say. This enables you to convey your character in a personal way. It follows fairly naturally that the delivery will be performed with like confidence.

One further case will reinforce the message that there are practical, cognitive ways to overcome self-doubt and carry confidence with you. The prospect of going live on radio would be daunting to most people. What makes it so is the thought of talking to a mass audience, perhaps amounting to hundreds of thousands. The approach of experienced announcers is to view the audience as an individual. In effect, they are sitting in front of a microphone talking to just one person. The announcers project themselves and relate one-to-one so that each individual in the audience is able to feel they are receiving special attention. Lose that touch, and you lose the audience.

This is a lesson that rings true for speeches. It feels good if you carry it off, and that is all the better for next time.

3. Speeches that hit the mark

They still shoot the messenger

The whole world's a stage, and there's a latent ability within us all to stand under the lights as one of its performers. All you have to do is assert that here I am and I have something to say—if not to the world, at least to your world. Examples abound from which we can draw helpful lessons from people who have made their mark on history to the galahs who have copped a 12 gauge where it hurts most and ended up a handful of feathers. Current experience as well as history tell us they still shoot the messenger.

The trick is to have confidence in your approach, and stay right out of range when things get ugly.

But first, how to get it right with a speech—to hit the mark—is an issue of many dimensions and variables. Among the questions that arise: How do you develop a speech that best fits with your speaker, yourself if you are the speaker, and the forum at which it's to be presented? How do you determine—and then achieve—the desired impact?

A good speech, no matter what level it's pitched at, ideally is a finely balanced mix of concepts and images that, supported by appropriate references, presents a holistic picture and makes for a damn fine story. It is important to appreciate the context of the speech as a messenger—what it is and its capabilities, and these fundamentals will help determine what you want to get out of a speech assignment and help in the way you frame it.

Many speakers continue to stick with the time-worn approach as a safety mantle—tell them what you're going to tell them, tell them, then tell them what you've told them. The format at the basis of this approach is to present a brief introduction, announce and outline the three key points the speaker is going to put forward, plough through the points in order, and finally reinforce them in summary form in the conclusion.

A known path to disaster

THE FORMULA SPEECH is akin to a yellow safety zone with a large crossing lady standing in the middle of it—as every kid with a survival instinct knows, the place you are most likely to get mown down by a four-wheel drive. There is a spot for the formula because it offers the security of a safe, known path for the speaker and many people are well versed in this means of presentation. But it falls way below Formula One. I much prefer to take them closer to the creative edge with a speech that aims to capture the imagination of the audience through a message presented in a way that touches their lives. I prefer a more creative, flowing style—a message that resonates with simple clarity and has the basic elements of a good story. There is nothing like a message that strikes a chord with your life's experience. There is nothing like a message that evokes the feeling deep within that, yes, that I can believe in, or, that inspires me. It has to be evocative and convincing in reaching heights that the formula speech can never attain.

The writer and speaker need to relate to people's experience, but seek to provide them with something more. You do not get your message across just by catching people's attention; you have to capture their imagination. They need something that reaches into their lives. And it must be right for the moment, and right for the particular audience. Yet clearly it must be the bearer of a message—a singular message supported by secondary points, or a sequence of two to four key inter-related points. The formula kind of speech does this. It is logically and methodically structured to reinforce a set of key precepts so that they sink in. But there are more creative ways of reaching the same end without it looking like the speech has come out of a textbook or is a recycled organisational presentation.

This makes a compelling case for the traditional full-text speech (as will be examined in detail when we come to look at the range of speech formats in Chapter 4). A full-text speech retains its place—a pride of place, I would argue—in the armoury of communication, and serves a valuable multi-purpose.

The differentiator

ONE OF THE KEY QUESTIONS about speechwriting is what is it that makes a great speech? We look to the examples from history for the answer. The American speechwriter and political columnist, William Safire, wrote in his book, *Lend Me Your Ears*, that often it is the occasion itself—the time when, as he said, '… someone is called upon to articulate the hope, pride or grief of all.'[1]

One of the great strengths of the traditional speech is that it maintains an important role in a social climate in which it might be seen to be pushing against a tide heading inexorably in the opposite direction. The speech is timeless. It originates from the pre-media grab era that is trending into commentary, much of it banal and predictable, and into infotainment and outright entertainment. It is an era in which people no longer talk in full sentences, but more in SMS speak, in which the language has been fundamentally debased, euphemisms are devised to hide real meaning, and people are judged on the style of their presentation rather than the content of what they are saying. There is fake sincerity in all of this, which goes a long way to explaining why people are so cynical about the pronouncements of politicians and business leaders.

A good, effective speech transcends these things. To pick up on Safire's point, most of the great speeches down history have risen from the cauldron of adversity. The great speeches find articulation out of oppression and tyranny, at times of grave danger, convey leadership, promise and hope, draw on the lessons of history, depict the dawn of a better future, and generally look beyond the immediate horizon. They mould people of a single mind. They are inspirational, aspirational and visionary.

Obviously, though, it is generally not demanded of us that we write the Ten Commandments or the Sermon on the Mount— and we have people like Gutenberg for his invention of a printing press using movable type around 1440 and, more recently, Bill Gates to thank that these things no longer need to be inscribed in stone or painstakingly handwritten on parchment. But still I insist that a good speech, however basic the topic, rises above the pedestrian level of day-to-day exchanges, and has an enduring quality.

Fellow Australian political speechwriter Don Watson asserts in his book on former Prime Minister Paul Keating the speech retains its ritual function. 'It remains the principal means of flesh-to-flesh contact between the politician and the people; it is the best means of framing the philosophical dimensions of a policy and often it provides an opportunity to set a new direction, create a new story, nail an opponent or massage one's way out of a predicament. A speech is a gesture towards order and respectability in a world which prizes spontaneity and tends towards chaos.'[2]

Watson is right—it is far from dead. In fact, there are more speeches being delivered today than ever before, from a far wider range of platforms than ever before. The days of people spruiking from soapboxes on street corners and politicking from the back of a truck or at a local church hall are no more. Maybe we are the worse for the passing of those raw and robust experiences, but the world moves on. Now the backdrops are staged political events and campaign launches, conferences, conventions, seminars, forums, launches, official openings, presentations, AGMs, internal corporate sessions, workplace briefings, protest rallies, citizenship ceremonies, and on and on.

And no longer is it predominantly the speaker who pens his or her own words. It is interesting to reflect that the practice of speechmakers employing other people to write their speeches on screens in lonely back rooms is a comparatively recent phenomenon. That makes good reason for communication professionals to position speechwriting high in their range of credentials. Here is an art form that requires practitioners.

As mentioned, the majority of great speeches have been born of adversity or challenge and the need for leadership and vision. It is instructive for modern day speechwriters to be familiar with them because they set the benchmarks and provide the legacy as a bridge into the environment in which we currently work. Notably, although time isolates them one from another, the common thread of history connects them. It is as if, as the Roman philosopher king, Marcus Aurelius, observed from his ruminations during his lengthy reign in the second century AD, '… the nature of the universe loves nothing so much as to change things which are and to make new things like them. For everything that exists is in a manner the seed of that which will be.' This is a defining statement that could well have emerged from an astute thinker in today's rapidly changing world. It lines up the guideposts to our endeavour to create a defining image within a speech, one that is all the more compelling if it is able to project the future on the basis of past and present experience. Marcus Aurelius, who stands alone in history for the very combination of qualities that made him the great philosopher king, is giving us the key: look at what exists today, at the direction to which it is pointing, and project it into the future. Look at what the thinkers out there are forecasting, and put your own definition on it.

The Marcus Aurelius quote fitted the mould of former Victorian Premier, Jeff Kennett, in that change and the nature and necessity of it were the foundations of his basic message, and I planned to use it in slightly extended form in one of his speeches. Up the corridor, the watchers of the political barometer ruled it out. It was probably as well because somewhere someone would have asked him who the hell is Marcus Aurelius? And ...

Great speeches for their time

INTERESTINGLY, IN 1997 the Melbourne Sunday Herald Sun ran as a centre page holiday filler a series of what it assessed as the great speeches of all time. The top five:

1. Jesus' Sermon on the Mount;
2. The Ten Commandments;
3. President Lincoln's Gettysburg Address;
4. Winston Churchill's 'We shall never surrender' speech in the Second World War; and
5. Martin Luther King's dream of a tolerant society address of 8 August 1963.

All are cries for hope out of adversity and oppression, so eloquently expressed in William Faulkner's brief acceptance speech for the Nobel Prize for Literature in 1950, 'I believe that man will not merely endure: he will prevail. He is immortal, not because he alone among creatures has an inexhaustible voice, but because he has a soul, a spirit capable of compassion and sacrifice and endurance.'

As in the cases of Lincoln and Churchill, war is often the rallying point for a good piece of oratory, and it has not always been men who have risen to the occasion. Elizabeth I rode to the port of Tilbury near the mouth of the Thames River in July 1588 to address a great crowd gathered there and the crews that would man an inferior English fleet against the formidable Spanish Armada amassing in the Channel. In a superb piece of rhetoric, framed within the emerging common language of her people, Elizabeth committed herself to them, her fate to theirs. 'I am come among you ... to live or die among you all; to lay down, for my God, and for my kingdom, and for my people, my honour and my blood, even the dust.'

Another usually quoted on the elite list is John F. Kennedy's 'Ask not what your country can do for you' speech at the Democratic Convention in 1960. Memorable, yes, but the words seem a bit cold and, well, political on paper all these years later. There is nothing of the style of King's abiding personal appeal for tolerance in his 'Free at Last' speech at the Lincoln Memorial in Washington on 28 August 1963, that rings with repetitions of, 'I have a dream ...,' and 'Let freedom ring ...' King was imploring Americans to dream with him, 'And so even though we face the difficulties of today and tomorrow, I still have a dream. It is a dream deeply rooted in the American dream. I have a dream that one day this nation will rise up and live out the true meaning of its creed: We hold these truths to be self-evident that all men are created equal.' He had returned to the roots of his nation—the Declaration of Independence of 1776—to assert the right to equality in modern day America.

Instead, I nominate another of Kennedy's speeches—from his presidential inauguration in January 1961—because it is timeless and provides a foretaste of the kind of sentiments world leaders would be expressing 40 years later towards the turn of the century:

> Let the word go forth from this time and place, to friend and foe alike, that the torch has been passed to a new generation of Americans—born in this century, tempered by war, disciplined by a hard and bitter peace, proud of our ancient heritage—and unwilling to witness or permit the slow undoing of those human rights to which this nation has always been committed and to which we are committed today at home and around the world.

His brother, Senator Robert Kennedy, was at least his equal for oratory that captured the national mood and the people's aspirations. It is widely held, rightly I believe, that he would have offered even greater promise for the future of America and the world than JFK. This capability is encapsulated in Robert Kennedy's address in Indianapolis on 4 April 1968, the night Martin Luther King was assassinated in Memphis:

My favourite poem, my — my favourite poet was Aeschylus. And he once wrote:

Even in our sleep,

Pain which cannot forget falls drop by drop upon the heart,

Until, in our own despair, against our will,

Comes wisdom through the awful grace of God.

What we need in the United States is not division; what we need in the United States is not hatred; what we need in the United States is not violence and lawlessness, but is love, and wisdom, and compassion towards one another, and a feeling of justice toward those who still suffer within our country, whether they be white or whether they be black ... the vast majority of white people and the vast majority of black people in this country want to live together, want to improve the quality of our life, and want justice for all human beings that abide in our land. And let's dedicate ourselves to what the Greeks wrote so many years ago: to tame the savageness of man and make gentle the life of this world. Let us dedicate ourselves to that, and say a prayer for our country and for our people.

And one that impresses a man's and his nation's revolutionary mark on history is from Nelson Mandela, 2 February 1990, when, on his release from prison, he proclaimed his vision for South Africa: '... apartheid has no future. It has to be ended by our own decisive mass action in order to build peace and security ... Our march to freedom is irreversible.' And Mandela echoed the sentiment of Martin Luther King, declaring 'Free at last' on his election as President of South Africa and the end of the regime of apartheid in 1994.

Among more recent American leaders (and that, like it or not, is the main global game and where the most poignant messages are coming from), the two standouts are Presidents George Bush Sr and Bill Clinton.

Although it is not generally recognised, George Bush Sr assembled one of the most talented speechwriting teams of any world leader in the latter part of the 20th century, to be matched only by those of Clinton and Britain's Tony Blair. And we can place Bush Sr to good effect in an Australian context, addressing the Federal Parliament in January 1992 to honour the 50th anniversary of the decisive battle of the Coral Sea.

> Of course, we've always shared fraternal ties and a spirit of freedom ever since an American vessel named Philadelphia became the first trading ship to call at Sydney's Port Jackson in 1792. Almost a century later, Mark Twain visited Australia and spoke for all Americans when he said: "You have a spirit of independence here which cannot be overpraised."

Remember that for when we come to deal with creating links and images in Chapter 8.

And in the same speech, Bush on the common spirit of the two Pacific allies:

And 50 years ago in the Coral Sea, Australians and Americans paid a high price for freedom, but they proved to the world that the future belongs to the brave and the bold. For the half century since, we have deepened our friendship, our economic interdependence and our collaboration on mutual defence. And now, more clearly than ever, we can see a hopeful future for the far-flung kinsmen of Australia and America and for all who share those fundamental ideals that we hold dear.

And to some notable lines from President Bill Clinton, which, as observed, take up and adapt some of the sentiments expressed by earlier presidents, particularly Kennedy and Bush Sr. From Clinton's Inaugural Address of January 1993 upon his first-term election:

Today, a generation raised in the shadows of the Cold War assumes new responsibilities in a world warmed by the sunshine of freedom but threatened still by ancient hatreds and new plagues. Raised in unrivalled prosperity, we inherit an economy that is still the world's strongest, but is weakened by business failures, stagnant wages, increasing inequality, and deep divisions among our people … Profound and powerful forces are shaking and remaking our world, and the urgent question of our time is whether we can make change our friend and not our enemy.

From Clinton's Inaugural Address in January 1997, drawing parallels that again conclude with a challenge suggesting there is, after all, an answer to all the trouble in the world:

Now, for the third time, a new century is upon us, and another time to choose. We began the 19th century with a choice, to spread our nation from coast to coast. We began the 20th century with a choice, to harness the industrial revolution to our values of free enterprise, conservation, and human decency. Those choices made all the difference. At the dawn of the 21st century a free people must now choose to shape the forces of the information age and the global society, to unleash the limitless potential of all our people and, yes, to form a more perfect union … The challenge of the past remains the challenge of our future—will we be one nation, one people, with one common destiny, or not? Will we all come together, or come apart?

Clinton addressing the Australian Parliament, 20 November 1996, in which he also invoked the memory of the visit of the good ship Philadelphia:

> For the first time in all history, two-thirds of all the nations on this earth and more than half the people alive today are ruled by governments picked by their own people. The rigid blocks and barriers that too long defined the world are giving way to an era of breath-taking expansion of information technology and information. And because of these things we now have a chance, greater than any generation of people who ever lived before us, to give more and more people the opportunity to realise their God-given potential to live their own dreams, not someone else's plan.

Further on, he spoke of globalisation and the joint responsibilities of Australia and America in Asia Pacific:

> Progress, after all, is not yet everyone's partner, and we have a responsibility to open the doors of opportunity to those who remain outside the global economy. For example, some two-thirds of the people on our planet have no access to a telephone. I found that hard to believe when I saw so many of your fellow citizens with their cellphones in their hands as I drove up and down your streets. More

than half the people of the world are two days walk from a telephone. They are totally disconnected from the communications and information revolution that is the present vehicle for human progress and possibility. If we add their creative energies to the mix which now exists, of course they will gain skills and jobs and greater wealth, but we also will benefit from the higher growth rates, from the expanded markets and from the increasing likelihood that those people will find peaceful rather than war-like ways to release their energies. We can do this if we have the courage not to retreat but instead to compete.

And a year beyond his presidency, delivering the 2001 Dimbleby Lecture, entitled 'The Struggle for the Soul of the 21st Century':

They (the 9/11 terrorists) thought that the differences they have with us, political and religious, were all that mattered and served to make all their targets less than human. Most of us believe that our differences are important and make our lives interesting but that our common humanity matters more. The clash between these two views over this simple question more than any other single issue, will define the shape and the soul of this new century.

In contrast, outstanding Australian examples are sparse, despite our colourful background, the adversities we have faced in a country that has shown its intransigent inhospitality to settlers who were not covered in fur or prickles, and the events that have built up that indefinable quality we are prone to call the Australian legend.

One that is entrenched in Australian history came from Prime Minister Ben Chifley in a 1949 address defining the objective of the Labour movement (before it became Labor) in the phrase, light on the hill:

> I try to think of the Labour movement, not as putting an extra sixpence into somebody's pocket, or making somebody Prime Minister or Premier, but as a movement bringing something better to the people, better standards of living, greater happiness to the mass of the people. We have a great objective—the light on the hill—which we aim to reach by working for the betterment of mankind not only here but anywhere we may give a helping hand.

The conservative Prime Minister Menzies is remembered for a populist term he used in a radio broadcast in May 1942, a description most often misrepresented as the 'forgotten people':

> In a country like Australia the class war must always be a false war. But if we are to talk of classes, then the time has

come to say something of the forgotten class—the middle class—those people who are constantly in danger of being ground between the upper and the nether millstones of the false class war; the middle class who, properly regarded, represent the backbone of this country.

Then, expounding on the theme in everyday terms:

I do not believe that the real life of this nation is to be found either in great luxury hotels and the petty gossip of so called fashionable suburbs, or in the officialdom of organised masses. It is to be found in the homes of people who are nameless and unadvertised, and who, whatever their individual religious conviction or dogma, see in their children their greatest contribution to the immortality of their race. The home is the foundation of sanity and sobriety; it is the indispensable condition of continuity; its health determines the health of society as a whole.

Mediocrity: stating the obvious

BUT THE FEW MEMORABLE Australian utterances are far exceeded by a string of real clangers and examples that have been either meaningless or mediocre, or both.

Take the momentous event of Federation in Australian history, a comparatively understated Down Under version of the American Declaration of Independence 125 years previously, that took no war to achieve, rather a spirited debate lasting some 40 years and the occasional biffo like the Eureka Stockade uprising along the way, and accommodated everyone but the indigenous people and women, with the singular exception of the Queen of England. This was payback time. After all, it was Her (Queen Victoria's) House of Commons that in 1850 passed an Act allowing the Australian colonies to be called States and granting them 'responsible government', one of the great political euphemisms of history that misguidedly endures to this day.

As the Federation debate warmed up, Edmund Barton, who was to be the first Prime Minister, declared at a meeting in Ashfield, New South Wales, in 1893, 'For the first time in history, we have a nation for a continent and a continent for a nation.' It may have sounded fine to the people in the hall at the time, but on paper after all these years looks the trite statement it actually was. More pertinent and resonant was the call from the Father of Federation, Sir Henry Parkes, at the 1891 Federation Convention, 'Are we not one people … one destiny?' that was to become the theme of the Federation movement. Better still the assertion of the man who was to be the second Prime Minister, Alfred Deakin, who saw in the creation of the Commonwealth of Australia the means to create the political embodiment of nationhood: 'The Commonwealth Constitution will begin to take effect on the 1st of

January (1901), but everything which could make the union it establishes more than a mere piece of political carpentry will remain to be accomplished afterwards.' And that is a challenge Australians are still coming to terms with, and it could well be because nothing like the same calibre of rhetoric emerged in the stumbling republican debate during the 1990s with the approach of the centenary of Federation.

Prime Minister Bob Hawke will be remembered as much for the doozie of all comments on child poverty as for the post-prime ministerial images of him and his new bride sporting white dressing gowns on a beach in Queensland. In his June 1987 election campaign address, Hawke got carried away in the belief that rhetoric and reality are one and the same. All it needs is to be said. 'Labor in Government has already taken major steps to tackle the great problem of children in poverty. We have already increased family payments to children in need by up to 70 percent. However, today Labor is going further. Labor is proposing major reform of the income support regime for low-income families. We pledge that by 1990 no child will need to live in poverty.' That last line haunted him through the remainder of his government.

The Prime Minister from 1996, John Howard, may not have been so outrageous, but he reinvented the whole communication relationship to the point where it became meaningless. Back in his opposition days, Howard sought to convey the conservative Coalition's philosophy with a series of addresses that he called 'headland speeches'. But if you were

36

looking for something like 'We'll fight them on the beaches', forget it. That came later on the waters far out in the Indian Ocean, and it was neither pretty nor edifying. He also coined the term 'mainstream Australia' as if it was to cement his credentials with everyday Australians. At one time while I was Jeff Kennett's speechwriter, Kennett asked me to come up with a new, defining, catchy description to replace the well-worn reference to 'ordinary Australians'. After a month or so, I came to the view there isn't one. Look to America if we must: there they call them, simply, Americans.

I love a rain-drenched country

Now, a Beware: Man-eating Dog warning for anyone who might be inclined to turn a poetic hand. Do not even try. If you must quote poetry, pinch someone else's and preferably someone who is good at it. John Gorton, the 60s PM with the face like a relief map of the Mekong Delta, is more than enough reason why.

Amid a timely spring downpour, Gorton officially opened the 1968 agricultural show at Hamilton in the south-west of Victoria with a poem obviously of his own hand, and he was known to like the odd drink or 30 which may have had something to do with it:

It isn't raining for me,

It's raining on the ground;

And in every dimple drop I see

More fodder around.

The Sydney Morning Herald panned the poem the following day. Gorton's minders responded by denying he had even quoted it. I was the local newspaper scribe who covered his speech and dug my heels in to defend my faltering shorthand account. Keith Dunstan, author of the celebrated 'A Place in The Sun' column in the Melbourne Sun, was not one to see a colleague discredited out of hand and came to my defence the next day. Dunstan questioned how Gorton's old alma mater, Oxford, where he gained a Master of Arts, would regard the verse. The lesson: for the likely impact of amateurish poetry, read that it creates a reaction like that of a like lead balloon.

It's Time to stand the test of time

THE STANDOUT AUSTRALIAN SPEAKERS of more recent times were Labor leader, Gough Whitlam, who overturned 17 years' conservative rule in 1972 on the catchcry of 'It's time, which captured a nation's imagination and cemented the belief that necessary change was in the wind, and Paul Keating, and not only for his ripostes on the floor of the Parliament. Each was able to rise to the occasion, and they had speechwriters of the calibre to weave the magic—Graham Freudenberg and Don Watson respectively. And, of course, there was Kennett, one of the few leaders of the second tier of Australian government—Australia's equivalent of an American state governor—to make a mark nationally and internationally. His time at the helm overlapped that of Keating, and as a basic rule of thumb, significantly more of Kennett's speeches than Keating's (and certainly of the Keating successor, Howard) rated reproduction in edited form on the Op-Ed pages of the nation's major newspapers. But more of Kennett later.

We will look at some of the Keating rhetoric that meets the standard of excellence and bears the test of time. His eulogy at the funeral service of the Unknown Australian Soldier on 11 November 1993 (Remembrance Day and, incidentally, the anniversaries of the Governor-General's sacking of Gough Whitlam and the hanging of Ned Kelly), which comes very close to an acceptable definition of the Australian character in today's terms:

> The Unknown Australian Soldier whom we are interring today was one of those who, by his deeds, proved that real nobility and grandeur belongs, not to empires and nations, but to the people on whom they, in the last resort, always depend.
>
> That is surely at the heart of the ANZAC story, the Australian legend which emerged from the war. It is a

legend not of sweeping military victories so much as triumphs against the odds, of courage and ingenuity in adversity. It is a legend of free and independent spirits whose discipline derived less from military formalities and customs than from the bonds of mateship and the demands of necessity. It is a democratic tradition in which Australians have gone to war ever since.

This Unknown Australian is not interred here to glorify war over peace; or to assert a soldier's character above a civilian's; or one race or one nation or one religion above another; or men above women; or the war in which he fought and died above any other war; or one generation above any that has been or will come later.

The Unknown Soldier honours the memory of all those men and women who laid down their lives for Australia. His tomb is a reminder of what we have lost in war and what we have gained. We have lost more than 100,000 lives, and with them all their love of this country and all their hope and energy.

We have gained a legend: a story of bravery and sacrifice and, with it, a deeper faith in ourselves and our democracy and a deeper understanding of what it means to be Australian.

It is not too much to hope, therefore, that this Unknown Australian Soldier might continue to serve his country—he might enshrine a nation's love of peace and remind us that, in the sacrifice of the men and women whose names are recorded here, there is faith enough for all of us.

Secondly, a Keating speech to Parliament on the republican proposal, 7 June 1995:

The creation of an Australian republic can actually deliver a heightened sense of unity, it can enliven our national spirit and, in our own minds and those of our neighbours, answer beyond doubt the perennial question of Australian identity—the question of who we are and what we stand for. The answer is not what having a foreign Head of State suggests. We are not a political or cultural appendage to another country's past. We are simply and unambiguously Australian.

He concluded that same address:

The detail of the changes we propose may at first glance obscure the meaning of them. (But) the meaning is simple and, we believe, irresistible—as simple and irresistible as the idea of a Commonwealth of Australia was to the Australians of a century ago. The meaning then was a nation united in common cause for the common good. A nation which gave expression to the lives we lead together on this continent, the experience and hopes we share as

41

Australians. The meaning now is still a product of that founding sentiment—it is that we are all Australians. We share a continent. We share a past, a present and a future. And our Head of State should be one of us.

Flamboyance and tattered texts

OR IF YOU WANT TO GO FOR FLAMBOYANCE, try your own adaptation of one of these (and hope, but in vain, that no one will remember it):

- At the end of September, 1938, British Prime Minister Neville Chamberlain returned to London after reaching what was euphemistically called a pact with Hitler in Munich. From a first floor window at 10 Downing Street, Chamberlain waved a tattered piece of paper he'd obviously picked up somewhere in the Marienplatz. Declaring to the crowd below, 'I believe it is peace for our time,' he urged them '… to go home and sleep quietly in your beds.' One year later the United Kingdom, France, Australia and New Zealand declared war on Germany.

- Russian leader, Nikita Krushchev, kept the Cold War on deep chill at a sitting of the United Nations General Assembly on 23 September 1960 by heckling and thumping the table during an address by the British

Prime Minister, Harold Macmillan. When that didn't work, Krushchev removed his right shoe, brandished it at a speaker and pounded it on his desk. The echo went around the world.

- The Palestinian leader, Yasser Arafat, outfitted in the familiar rebel style with his trademark checked tea towel head-dress, upstaged Krushchev in an historic address to the UN General Assembly in New York on 13 November 1974, 'Today I have come bearing an olive branch and a freedom fighter's gun,' he said, brashly brandishing both.

Each of these events made front pages around the world. Each also had unforeseen and unintended consequences, not that they detracted in the least from the players or the theatre they created.

In Britain, it wasn't long before no one was sleeping well at night. There is no record unfortunately whether Krushchev was for real or had been into the vodka or if he subsequently had to dash into Macy's to buy a new pair of shoes. The Soviet Union ultimately decided disunion was the way to go, and now everyone wears Nikes. And in the third instance, what would have happened had the gun gone off and left olive branch fragments splattered on the ceiling of the General Assembly? Not that it would have made any difference. Arafat died in his checked tea towel—properly called a kefiyeh, as I found—and the Middle East is just as peaceful a place now as it was then.

Defining lines: the fourth estate

FROM POLITICS AND JOURNALISM, there sometimes emerges the coining of terms that have become part of the common language or are definitive in their simplicity. There is an ill-match among the succession of political 'gate' scandals that have been headlined regularly from the 1990s as latter day successors to Watergate, which was the actual name of the hotel where President Richard Nixon's right hand men and their hired thugs—i.e., the people running the country—broke into the Democratic Party's election HQ and gave credence to the subsequent naming of the scandal surrounding the break-in. Today the appendage 'gate' to signify a scandal is no more than the nondescript refuge of a new generation of reporters and sub-editors who read psychology or sociology and lack understanding of how the world came to be the way it is and the imagination to come up with something original and pertinent to the current event.

Looking to the defining terms, we find they go back a bit in time. I refer firstly to another of Churchill's statements, in which he coined a generational description that served in common use throughout the Cold War. On 3 March 1946, Churchill declared, 'From Stettin in the Baltic to Trieste in the Adriatic, an Iron Curtain has descended across the Continent.'

And the term Cold War itself was defined by American journalist Walter Lippman, who wrote a book called *Cold War* in 1947.

The language deployed in journalism is in serial decline, but there are examples of journalism that can be instructive in the way of writing speeches because they are both succinct and create exactly the image of the moment. The one most thumbed among my crammed files of newspaper clippings dating back to the 1950s is of a journalist writing about a speech. His twelve-word introduction probably tells us more than the speech ever could.

It is a time when the United States has experienced problems in stormy waters abroad and is overwhelmed by mounting domestic problems. Responding to this situation in his State of the Union address, President Nixon signals a switch from foreign to domestic policy. Writing in The New York Times of 23 January 1970, James Reston sums it up in the introductory paragraph to his column: 'President Nixon is bringing the ship of State back home for repairs.'[3]

Sportswriters, particularly Americans, have also exhibited the knack of capturing the atmosphere of big events. A wire service article datelined Kinshasa (Zaire, now capital of the Democratic Republic of the Congo), 29 October 1974, caught the mood of the final hours before the famed rumble in the jungle, the world heavyweight bout in which Muhammad Ali pounded

George Foreman to the canvas: 'The talking and pre-fight ballyhoo are almost over—and in a few hours George Foreman and Muhammad Ali will climb out of bed to try to knock each other unconscious under an African moon.'

Particularly note in the more outstanding examples that have been quoted how the speakers drew on history and linked it to their times and themes, their use of anecdotal references to bring their messages within the experience of everyday people, and the use of rhetoric that seeks to uplift. In these things are the makings of a memorable speech.

The couple of media articles exude imagery—incisive and colourful. That is what this traverse through history has been all about. Look at it in the context of the thinking of Peter Koestenbaum, who for the past quarter century has applied his expertise in philosophy to the relationship between business and people. As reported in Fast Company Magazine, 'His agenda: to apply the power of philosophy to the big question of the day—how to reconcile the often-brutal realities of business with basic human values—and to create a new language of effective leadership. "Unless the distant goals of meaning, greatness and destiny are addressed," Koestenbaum insists, "we can't make an intelligent decision about what to do tomorrow morning—much less set a strategy for a company or a human life. Nothing is more practical than for people to deepen themselves."'[4]

4. Speech formats

A speech can take one of four formats:

1. Full text—with the intention the speaker will read it and stick to the text;

2. Extensive text, but incorporating dot points in some areas that the speaker is able to talk generally around;

3. An extended dot point format where the points are actually sentences but serve to give the speaker wider scope to talk around them; or

4. Shorthand dot points—points that are not full sentences, but provide the speaker with prompts or headlines.

The question—to which there is no set formula answer—is how to work out which format is right for a particular occasion. But the way to determine the best course to take is to assess the speaker—their thoughts, requirements, grasp of the subject, their approach to the speaking engagement, their ability and experience in handling a public performance—along with the nature of the forum where they are to appear and the level of public and media interest in the event. A further factor is whether what is said will become a matter of public record and/or is likely to be published or circulated.

Full text

IN WHAT CIRCUMSTANCES would you write a full-text speech—and, importantly, for it to be understood the speaker sticks to the text? Some examples will provide a guideline:

- If they were addressing the National Press Club, unquestionably yes—full text that is well rehearsed in advance, accompanied by comprehensive briefing notes and a question and answer backgrounder;
- Industry conferences and conventions, from which the organisers are likely to require texts to distribute later to delegates or publish in their newsletters;
- Similarly, government-hosted events;
- Specific issue seminars where there will be a line-up of speakers who will be presenting different perspectives on an issue or even debating it;

- Company/organisation annual general meetings and results briefings to analysts and the media;

- Major corporate announcements or launches;

- Representing the company/organisation in hostile environments, such as protest rallies, or at public meetings with interest/activist groups in attendance and where an issue of public concern is at stake; and

- At events that are of significant public interest and likely to result in extensive media coverage.

First timers and people who are called on only infrequently to speak should always develop a full script. It is the essential insurance policy that helps keep the confidence level up and avoids the risk of a memory block should there be a momentary panic attack. And maybe pack a couple of valium! But never resort to alcohol as a prop. Even a seemingly harmless single glass of wine can have the effect of inducing elephantiasis of the tongue and it will reflect in the performance. In situations where pre-event drinks are served or there is a dinner accompanied by drinks before the speech is scheduled, be the one that, as Rudyard Kipling said, keeps their head while all about them are losing theirs.

Extensive text

THE SECOND FORMAT uses extensive text with some guideline points in part—that is, it allows scope in places for the speaker to extemporise.

This could still be an industry related forum, a corporate announcement or significant corporate function, or a launch type of event.

The test here is that the core messages are set out in text, but it is accepted the speaker has sufficient grasp of the subject to be able to talk around the related issues, examples and case studies, and to explain the applications, implications and potential of particular developments or trends without the need for recourse to a full text.

Extended dot points

THE USE OF A SPEECH with extended dot points—our third category—is a bit more difficult fit. It is heading towards the halfway mark—a speech where you set out sentences as dot points, but that are guidelines for a speaker in a situation that may still be formal and yet is not so critical and comes under less scrutiny and public attention than the first two. Nevertheless, it is a good idea to spell out the two or three key quote paragraphs and messages that may be repeated for emphasis.

Generally, this format will be for speeches of shorter duration—around the 10-minute mark is a good guide.

This allows the speaker to talk around the points, to be more engaging and friendly with the audience. It could apply to a launch or corporate announcement, but is more appropriate to the type of event where the speaker is representing the company as host for a function, or is there as the sponsor.

Shorthand dot points

AGAIN, THERE IS SOME OVERLAP down this pyramid when we look at the use of shorthand dot points—a one- to three-page set of guideline points that are not in sentence form, but serve as prompts.

This could also apply to situations where an organisation is hosting or sponsoring an event, where the speaker has an introductory or lead-in role to the main event, or if their task is to respond with a toast or thank you at the end of the program.

The dot-point format has a further use in providing guidelines for the delivery of presentations backed by extensive graphics that might provide a corporate and industry overview or, say, to announce and explain a new corporate direction or a development in technology. It would be suitable for informal or background briefings, or internally for briefings on structural and technological changes, or for presenting business performance assessments.

In this case, your speaker knows what the message is. All they need are the headlines to keep it in order. Again, it is most likely to be for a speech of short duration or one that is delivered in a comparatively informal environment.

The determining factor

THE SPEAKER is a primary consideration in determining the format.

Some people simply are not comfortable without a full text. Some like more flexibility—to have the main quotes set out in full, along with any supporting statistics, but to have their key points headlined and summarised. They know their subject and/or are prepared to devote the time to think through their message and take in the briefing papers on the particular issue and event. Being well prepared and having confidence in being in the spotlight, they are more at ease being able to talk around the summarised points and feel it gives them greater scope to engage the audience.

These are people who are experienced, what you might call natural public performers who come across all the more forcefully without the constraint of having to read a set piece. Some people read well from text, especially if they have fully rehearsed it, but some find it confines their style.

There is another variation in this same mould—the ones who like to have text, but to have it in a tightly written summary form. They will use the text, but expand on it, particularly in the areas where they are elaborating on their key points.

And there are times, much to the chagrin of the writer who has sweated at length over the text, when the speaker determines to wing it or maybe has some other agenda in mind. Countless times walking into a function with Victorian Premier Kennett he would hand back the speech folder and say, I won't be needing this. At that point you never knew what to expect.

The situation where you have a speaker who will talk around a text also has implications for the timing of it. If they are programmed for 25 minutes, you need to work out roughly how long they might talk on their own account and cut the text back accordingly. Timing, though, is another matter that we will go into later on.

As examples, I used a combination of shorthand and extended dot points—points that flowed logically and spelt out the messages—for former Telstra Chief Executive Dr Ziggy Switkowski and Telstra Director Catherine Livingstone at the 2003 Telstra Women's Business Awards' presentation. They were part of a long line-up of speakers and we had to remember people's main reason for being there was to find out who were the winners. Ziggy therefore focused on Telstra's sponsorship as a means to recognise and promote the achievements of women and the value to the entrants of the experience of the awards process. Director Livingstone's key points were on innovation, women in education and women in small business. In each case, short, sharp and to the point.

For major events such as the World IT Congress that Dr Switkowski addressed in 2002 and for keynote addresses to national industry functions, we consistently used full text. The same was the case with keynote speeches for Premier Kennett, such as his address to the Constitutional Convention in Canberra, to the Asia Society in New York and his various Menzies and Deakin lectures. If in contrast he was opening a factory or art show or announcing a new investment or talking to a school assembly, he would have been armed with dot points providing no more than the basic, salient information and a background outline on the organisation or occasion and the make-up of the audience. He had more than enough presence to tell a story, often one that came totally unexpected to the speechwriter and advisers travelling with him.

Summary

You will arrive at the right format option by making an assessment that takes account of the occasion, the nature of the address and the preference of your speaker.

There is just one note of caution to take into account. Enabling a speaker to talk around a subject leaves open the possibility they will get carried away and drop a clanger. Jeff Kennett used to describe the surprise element as 'tossing a dead cat on the table'. Sometimes it was a dead possum. The effect was the same.

Nevertheless, your speaker should be clear that the last thing you want is for the media office or the rest of the organisation to have to spend the next week digging you out of a no-win hole.

Powerpoint

That brings us to consider the specifics of presentations, which, like meetings, have taken over organisational practice and generally rely for their effect on extensive packages of Powerpoint slides. I don't much like the term presentation for a start. It's one of those catchwords that have crept into the lexicons of government, business and academia. But sometimes it is hard to escape.

I have an even greater dislike of Powerpoints, principally because they are so rarely used to effect. Mostly, they are a prop that distracts attention from the speaker, or a graphic device that tells the audience at a glance what the speaker is going to say while they labour on saying it long after the message has sunk in—a sure-fire way to create the conditions for a series of power naps (a whole new audience concept here potentially—Powerpoint naps!).

Powerpoint is a latter day echo of the old edict of television news in the era before the network people and presenters woke up that their audience could actually see the pictures. The principle was that the script had to follow the pictures to the split second. This was the basis of a classic send-up on the David Frost show going back some decades. It got to the point, Frost said, where if a BBC reporter referred to the title Lord Privy Seal, viewers would be shown a rapid sequence of three pictures—a Lord, a toilet, and a seal.

Powerpoints, though, do have a place in illustrating graphically the point a speaker is making, in pictorial or diagrammatic format, or in listing for the audience's reference the core points they are explaining. But it takes good planning to work well. Telstra had a graphic called the Spaghetti Slide, which its people were fond of including in the CEO's and divisional chiefs' presentations. The slide showed a mass of small inter-linked yellow blobs, each listing a factor in the complex regulatory environment for the Australian telecommunications industry. Looking at it was like trying to read a message in a plate of spaghetti. And that was the point—to illustrate a confusing maze. It is essential to think about, and question, what is really needed, whether it helps or adds anything to the overall message or specific elements of it.

More recent and more versatile versions of Powerpoint, like the one in the Office 2004 suite on my Mac, provide greater scope to liven up a presentation. But even given that, I would be more inclined to use it as a distraction with a mix of graphics, video and audio that a speaker can call on periodically to inject an unexpected element or some humour into a presentation. The kind of thing that comes way out of left field.

To reinforce my point, the use of Powerpoint was debated in companion articles in the September 2003 edition of Wired Magazine in an article adapted from separate articles written by David Byrne and Edward Tufte.

Artist and musician, David Byrne, put the case in favour in a sarcastic kind of way, arguing the medium is the message. Its capability to make hilariously bad-looking visuals, he said, is a small price to pay for ease and utility. Byrne took it so far as to make presentations about presentations. They were almost completely without content because, as he learned, the content is in the medium itself. What's more, the application can be made to run by itself—no one even needs to be at the podium.[5]

Yale infographic guru, Edward Tufte, put the opposing case with a fundamental message: 'Power corrupts. Powerpoint corrupts absolutely.' Tufte claims the Powerpoint style routinely disrupts, dominates and trivialises content. His findings are: one, that rather than supplementing a presentation, Powerpoint has become a substitute for it; and, two, that this ignores the most important rule of speaking: respect your audience.[6]

In other words, if you must use them, be restrained, discerning and creative in the way that you do.

5. Know the context

The starting point is to establish the nature of the function at which a speech is to be delivered, or the circumstances in which a presentation is to be made, in infinite detail. There is to be no putting pen to paper or words on a screen until this initial investigation is done and every aspect is set out in logical order. This will help put in place the guideposts to follow.

The elements involved in establishing the context:

- Gain a comprehensive rundown of the organisation running the event or forum, which is generally readily available on the Internet, although it is also important to put in a call to discuss with someone connected with the event what they are on about and set up a point of liaison as a source of information and someone you can keep tabs with on the specific arrangements;

- Alternatively, if it is an internal event or meeting where reports or presentations are to be delivered within your own organisation, seek out the organiser and work with them on that same basis;

- From your research and direct approach, develop a profile of the organisation—what it is, how long it has been going, what it does, what it believes in, the key people behind it, the make-up of its membership, its areas of activity and influence. Often, in conversation with organisers, you will pick up a quote that crystallises the nature of an organisation and what it is about. Your speaker can use that to great effect to show an understanding of them the way they see themselves. In other words, establish rapport by depicting them in their own image;

- Get details of the event and the program and who is attending, and where your organisation and your speaker fit into it, and how much time has been allocated for your speaker;

- Obtain a list of people who should be formally acknowledged—and check their titles and the spelling of their names as per one of the primary rules of journalism: get their titles and names right as a matter of cardinal respect;

- Establish the purpose of the event and the reason for your involvement and what they expect of you;

- Get an indication of what other speakers are saying to dovetail the speaker's message with theirs—and it is generally helpful to talk directly with them;

- Do they have a suggested title for the speech, or are they leaving it up to you? And if they have a title, make sure you are at ease with it. The option is always open to put forward a variation, or to work the speech around it in a way that subtly enables you to develop it around on the message you want to get across;

- Get a rundown on the venue layout and the facilities that will be available—if it is to be onstage behind a lectern, if you're able to use graphics;

- Establish the logistics—where the speaker is to arrive, who will meet them, what is expected of them throughout the program and when they can reasonably expect to get away; and

- Finally, get an indication of what the organisers are doing to promote the event and whether you might be able to provide some positive input into that in association with them or on your own account. And establish if they are anticipating wider public interest beyond their membership, in particular whether the media will be there and what wider circulation the speech may be given.

The compilation of these very basic things gives you invaluable guidelines for your planning and preparation. Moreover, they define the most critical component in the whole exercise— your audience and the nature of the potentially extended audience.

6. Know your speaker

Maybe you are the one at centre-stage, the one who has to write and stand and deliver. In that case, you know the language you are comfortable with. Write what is right for you. Present your ideas and the kind of image in which you see things. Instil it with your character and sense of humour. Picture it from the point of view that you want to engage with people on your terms, from your perspective, to tell them your story but in a way that relates to them.

But if you are writing for someone else, you need to know them. There are ways of doing this effectively. Pick up their style of talking—from speeches they have delivered before and media transcripts, from hearing them address staff gatherings or talking around the office, talking to them on the phone or in person. If it is possible, try to sit down with them at an early stage in the assignment and get them to outline how they see the speech, what they are thinking in the context of it, the main messages they believe should emerge, the way they describe things. Alternatively, you can get the sense of the message from the people who are close to them and have ready access to them. One way or another you will discern their footprints in the sands of time.

Lend a sharp ear in your discussion with them or your reading of what they have said before for recurrent words, phrases, descriptions, the images they use to depict the way they see things, their grasp of multi-syllable words and technical terms. Try to discern the words they don't use or that don't fit with their terminology. I once used the word 'exponentially' in a speech for Jeff Kennett, which in the translation came out as 'tremendous'. Ok, take heed that exponential is not part of his lexicon. Just like he had to be coached for three days to pronounce 'inviolable', as in inviolable rights, for his suggested new Preamble to the Australian Constitution. But it stayed in because it was crucial to the intent of the statement and he played it up with some pride on radio on the launch day. In essence, what you hear from your speaker is what they are comfortable with, a verbal window on their character and thinking. Use it.

Working in relative isolation

THE QUESTION OF KNOWING YOUR SPEAKER has thrown up a quandary that has often been raised with me in discussions about speechwriting—the problem of working in relative isolation. Given their schedules, it is often difficult to get close to a senior executive and then to get them for more than a minute or two, even for people working within the office. And it can be just as difficult to get the feedback you need to advance from either your initial outline notes or the first draft. With this situation as the norm, the speechwriter's over-riding challenge is that of being able to put words into someone else's mouth that reflect their ideas and sound like them.

The way to bridge the gap is through your approach and with the support of the organisation around you. It is achieved by dealing with the speaker directly whenever possible, but more often indirectly through the people who are close to them and by looking at records of what they have said.

The organisation can generally be relied upon as a source of background information and a reference point to external sources. Talk to the people who talk to the chief. They can get the chief's ear easier than you can. They know the organisation's position and whether there are any touchy issues currently out on the street, or impending, that you need to be aware of. They know the projects that are in the pipeline that might be worth a mention. They have a perspective of the interests of the business divisions within the organisation and the avenues within those to find the information you need.

It is possible to function effectively and professionally and keep a firm hand on the tiller in either environment—where you have full or extensive access, or if you are in solitary confinement. The result will be your carefully and imaginatively crafted speech in terms that are as near as can be the natural expression of your speaker.

Timing the speech

TWO OTHER FACTORS fall within the ambit of knowing your speaker. The first is their talking speed. Radio newsreaders with the BBC and ABC have traditionally been trained to talk at 180 words a minute, three words a second, and that is how they time the bulletins. The average public speaker is in the 140 to 150 words a minute range. I generally write to a target around the 140 mark or a little higher for speeches. I take into account that the initial acknowledgements may well run longer than the word count indicates, there may be time out for applause or hecklers, and it is rare for a practised speaker not to add in an extra comment periodically through the delivery.

The second factor is to establish the format—whether, as dictated by the occasion and the preference of the speaker, it is full text or any of the other format variations we went through earlier.

This also influences the quantity of text you provide. Where for a 25-minute engagement the speaker wants extended text with scope to talk around summary points, you would cut the word count back to fifteen to eighteen minutes. In making this determination, it helps no end to establish the speaker's preference, either from them or someone who is close to them.

7. Know your subject

A tour of discovery

The importance of getting a thorough handle on the subject goes without saying. But here we are going to cut to the chase and set out a research method that will gather exactly the information you need in the shortest possible time. There are two ways of conducting research—this lean and hungry, time-effective way, or getting bogged down in reams of irrelevant information and statistics and following search paths that lead nowhere in particular.

You can end up with such a volume of peripheral information that it becomes confusing and that makes it difficult to pinpoint the key messages and direction of the speech, and it is a waste of time. In writing speeches for company executives, it is common for the corporate affairs, PR and media areas to provide whatever information they may have readily available and canvass around the appropriate business divisions for whatever current and background papers and presentations they are able to contribute. That often results in a flood of email attachments and/or couriered material that could run to around 200 pages, sometimes more. Overload. But I don't object to that so much. I would rather have their contributions promptly volunteered than have to dig through concrete to get it.

This may seem a contradiction to the time-effective method I am leading into. With experience, though, it is possible to set some parameters in your own mind. The way to go is to scan that information (on-screen is the best way) and copy and paste only what fits the defined parameters into your initial planning document. And take summary notes only from hard copy material strictly on the basis of relevance. You emerge from the exercise with a range of references that will be disordered at this stage, but will have had the effect of cutting 200 pages down to no more than five. The practice of on-screen scanning where possible—the paperless approach—is important because it is the fastest method and cuts the original information overload down to a workable set of references. Print it out and you will have to read the lot and waste time making your own notes, and you will tend to overdo the note-making. What's more, the on-screen method means the information is contained within an electronic document where it can be cut and moved around to put it in logical order or readily copied into the appropriate places in the synopsis or the draft, ready to be moulded into the text. Just one cautionary note here: it is important to reference each piece of information so that you are able to support statements and statistics drawn from external sources. Often an organisation will query where a particular piece of information came from, or it could be questioned in the course of the speaking engagement or in subsequent media interviews. Sometimes it may be pertinent to footnote the references within the speech, but generally it is not necessary to put them in the speech text. However, the writer should provide a separate list of sources in case the organisation or speaker is called on to substantiate statements or figures posed as factual. It may also be the case that material from the speech is later recycled into other speeches or documents, in which event the references will establish the veracity of the information. The speech may also be published in hard copy or on the organisation's web site, or indeed become an academic reference, and in each of these cases the sources should be included as footnotes or endnotes.

The context of the function or event and the background on the organisation and people connected with it, detailed in Chapter 5 as the starting point for the speech, will provide a valuable basis for some workable ideas and lines. Aside from the information on the organisation's web site, it may well be able to provide you with some helpful background or issues papers.

Should it happen that you are delivering an address or lecture scheduled annually to honour the organisation's founder or its mission, an early step is to look at the titles and read the texts of at least the last three memorial lectures, documents that generally are available on the Net.

Fast and lean research

THE RESEARCH METHOD involves a tour of discovery internally and outside the speaker's own organisation. Importantly, it also reaches into the detail of the subject or subjects you will cover and the broader environment within which they are set. That might be an industry sector, the field in which the organisation operates, or, for an individual, the interests and ideas you want to project, and it might be in an Australian, regional or totally global context, or come from an entirely personal perspective.

For corporate speakers, the writer needs to know company policy and strategy, what the respective business units or departments within the organisation are doing in relevant fields, what is in the planning pipeline that could possibly make for a new announcement, and most importantly seek out the successful things that other people in the organisation have been said before, even that people in the same industry sector or relevant government people have said before.

These can be used or adapted to good effect, and help ensure the message is consistent. And there will always be the core philosophy, direction and basic messages that position an organisation and need to be repeated and reinforced. Take a lesson from the advertising industry, but pull back from all-out hype and take the subtle line. Do not always repeat the corporate mantras as a matter of course. Speeches are not necessarily a hard logo or brand sell. In fact, over-sell can turn people off.

The extensive range of resources that can be drawn upon in what should be a comprehensive research program incorporate:

- Your own knowledge bank, i.e. background knowledge of the topic, and the ideas you develop around it;

- The company's or organisation's position and what has been said on the topic, or topics, previously;

- By extension, documents like the annual report, presentations developed for shareholders, analysts, the media and/or interest groups and supporters, presentations that have been developed internally, and material on the organisation's Internet site and Intranet;

- The viewpoints of the speaker, the people around them and the company's business units or the divisions of the organisation;

- What outside people are saying on the subject and about the particular organisation; and

■ The position of the organisation your speaker is addressing—whether it is ambivalent or a single-issue lobby group or a group that represents a broad range of interests and holds strong views on a variety of issues.

Then set out on your own account to discover things, establish the links and piece it all together.

Other primary sources

THE AUSTRALIAN BUREAU OF STATISTICS (abs.gov.au) is a fundamental source of statistics, but also of economic and social studies and papers from almost any aspect imaginable. The AusStats area of the ABS site is a good place to start, and basic information can be accessed quickly under the Popular Statistics link. As an example as to how this information can be applied, if you know how many lion tamers there are in Australia and you would like to emphasise their rarity by expressing their number as a percentage of the national population, a link under AusStats' Popular Statistics will give an estimate of the Australian population as of the moment you click into that page. While the ABS presents a comprehensive social picture of the nation, the Australian Institute of Family Studies (aifs.gov.au) is an excellent reference point for social studies on subjects relating to the work-life balance, women, children, parenting and the changing nature of families.

The Australian Parliament's library (find it via aph.gov.au) is a rich source of study papers and archives and there are archives galore on the Parliament site. Additionally, the Hansard reports on the sites of the Australian Government and the States and Territories provide access to parliamentary proceedings extending back some decades, and all the government sites provide links into every area of government.

Depending on your needs, the United Nations (un.org), Organisation for Economic Co-operation and Development (oecd.org), the World Bank (worldbank.org) and the Oxford Journals (wber.oxford.journals.org) provide a wealth of information via their web sites. Much of their work has a global perspective, but there is also a good deal of comparative material with handy statistics and on issues covering single countries and the developed and undeveloped nations. And there are the sites of industry organisations—peak bodies such as the Business Council of Australia (bca.com.au), the Australian Chamber of Commerce and Industry (acci.asn.au) and Australian Institute of Management (aim.com.au), in particular its Australian Business Leader Surveys locatable under Research. Then there are the specific business sector organisations and a wide range of consulting and polling organisations that regularly conduct surveys and pull together statistical information in their field. For technical and scientific information, look to the CSIRO (csiro.au). And information of a general nature, covering almost every aspect of history and life in Australia, can be found in the Australian Stories Index (cultureandrecreation.gov.au/stories). To cover all the bases, also conduct a general Net search, taking a range of different angles with differing search strings.

I also keep tabs on a range of magazine related sites that publish not only their magazines but provide up-to-date news and features online. They include Wired (wired.com) and Fast Company (fastcompany.com) magazines, The Economist (economist.com) the excellent UK publication, Prospect Magazine (prospect-magazine.co.uk), and O Magazine produced by Oprah Winfrey. Among the online news and information outlets, go to news.google.com (news.google.com/news?ned=au for the Australian oriented version) for global news; the Drudge Report (drudgereport.com) for inside oil and commentary on just about everything; espn.com for anything to do with sport; and wikipedia.org for anything to do with anything. These are good sources because their focus is to find people thinking outside the square and new and futuristic ideas and they track changes in lifestyle trends and social thinking. For the latest on information and communications technology, look Wired, CNET News, and ZDNet, which has both global and Australian sites, and the high-tech links from Netscape's news service. Also do not overlook that there are many other points of view or points of conflict. Look therefore to alternative news sources such as the Australian crikey.com.au and, on major public issues and campaigns, to activist sites such as moveon.org and participate.net. And for something really out there, good for some light relief if nothing else, try the alternative, make-believe news service, The Onion News (theonion.com/content/index).

It should not, though, be a random trawl, but a targeted search for specific, pertinent information—information that fits and extends the dimension of the pattern you have in mind—as well as supporting statistics and forecasts. Otherwise you are losing valuable time, perspective and sense of direction.

Knowledge banks

IN RESPECT OF RESEARCH and information processing, I advocate the benefits for organisations of creating an internal, contributory, shared and readily accessible knowledge bank.

The balance sheet puts a value on an organisation—its property, plant and equipment, inventories, goodwill and so on. Intellectual property has a dollar value, but generally only where it has been patented. Only in rare instances do companies, any organisation for that matter, put a tangible value on their intangible accumulated knowledge, and it is from a lack of understanding that this is the one asset capable of propelling them into the future. Companies talk about people being their most important asset, but without knowing why and without endeavouring to aggregate their collective knowledge. It is not that they are nice to talk to, friendly, good public-spirited, church-going people, but because of what they know and how they apply their knowledge. And it multiplies in value as a pooled, accessible resource.

A growing number of organisations are taking positive steps towards aggregating the experience and knowledge that walks in and out of their doors each day and making it available to everyone within the organisation to use and to amend and extend as need be. The notion that knowledge is power is history. In fact, it is an assertion that dates back centuries to a time when books were not widely available. But how prevalent we find that antiquated, entirely self-centred and self-protective attitude in today's workplaces! Its practitioners are people who really should be taken out the back and shot. Ready accessibility to the organisational knowledge bank gives people an up-to-date picture of what the organisation is saying and doing, where it is heading and the ideas that are taking it there. It can be an invaluable short circuit in the preparation of speeches and presentations. Companies in Northern Europe pioneered the idea of putting a bottom line value on their internal knowledge and now the practice is spreading in America. Indeed, it is being extended beyond workplace practice and experience to the collection of stories people spread from workstation to workstation or exchange across their canteen lunch tables, stories that far more than any mission statement are the cultural basis of an organisation, that harbour a wealth of experience and know-how and paint an evolutionary picture that can be made dynamic and serve as a guide to the future. Collating and aggregating this knowledge and information is a trend that smart managements are picking up. But as we enter an era in which different, creative-oriented skills and the capability for innovative ideas are coming to the fore, it will become the mark of success. Those intractable organisations and people that deny its value and power are doomed by their shortsightedness and outdatedness.

This has been slow to happen because of the territorialism factor—the silo mentality that prevails in many organisations and the divide between management and the shop floor. There is also the problem of time constraints that put knowledge sharing down the priority order.

But it is important and requires the calibre of people who are prepared to say we need to think and operate differently. This approach it can work wonders.

8. Planning and writing

From this point, we head into the main game. With the background checks and research completed, we embark on the procedure to put the information in order, develop an outline plan or synopsis and write the first draft. This stage will take the writer through the need initially to establish and have a clear focus on the objective of the speech, and throughout to stay on message and demonstrate that they know and respect the audience. It will cover mastery of the language and detail the most effective techniques for writing the spoken word. There are hints and examples showing how to create links and images that are at once out of the ordinary yet will hit the audience's connect button, as well as how to inject humour into a speech without appearing to be a clown. This will lead to Chapter 9, which sets out a range of case studies and examples, principally from my own experience and building on those cited in Chapter 3, to illustrate these points and inspire you to aspire to a fine style of writing—creative and uplifting, constructed with a sense of story that builds expectation, each point argued with a razor intellect.

At this point, writers will have accumulated a background document of five or six pages of research notes plus statistics in a computer file and maybe a few pages of handwritten notes, ideas and potential quotes. The next step is to follow a logical plan to put it into order in a synopsis that is a well-defined map of the direction the speech will take.

Developing the synopsis

First, head a separate document listing the title, event, speaker and date you will actually use in the speech itself, along these lines (I have the header in small capitals and venue and date lower case, but it is a matter of preference):

'Speech Title (if designated; if not, coin one)'
Speaker's Name and Title
Title of the Conference or Event
Sydney, 10 December 2007

Often, if there is to be media interest and the likelihood of the speaker straying from the text, a precautionary note, CHECK AGAINST DELIVERY, will be inserted flush left and in unbolded capitals above the heading. And page numbers should be inserted top right from the second page onward to guide the speaker.

Next, number and headline the main sections of the speech in bold type, leaving several line spaces between each of them:

Acknowledgments

Introduction

Key Point Summary

Key Point 1

Key Point 2

Key Point 3

Conclusion

There may be more than three key points, but you do not want to overload it.

I will digress a little to put this into an everyday context— the line-up of a television news bulletin. This is more relevant than a comparison with radio because the half hour TV news parallels a speech—the audience sees the speaker and hears the words, and can fully appreciate the manner of presentation. Seeing and hearing also implants the content more firmly in people's minds than happens when they merely hear a voice. As a test, sit through a radio and television news bulletin with someone, then ask them to recount the first three headlines. They may manage that from the visual connection with television, but you will win money every time on their recall from radio—maybe one headline, and not necessarily the main one.

The typical television news has three headline stories followed by a recap of the headlines. It moves then to a wrap-up of the other national news, the main overseas headline and an overseas wrap-up, a finance headline and summary, and to sport where there may be one or two headlines and a general wrap-up. There may be a human interest or offbeat story to conclude the bulletin after the weather, and the three top headlines will be summarised again, or there will be visual footage reinforcing the main headline story as the credits roll. Fundamentally, the bulletin is cast around three stories with supporting information that fills in the snapshot of the day. It is a thoroughly market researched format, and it works.

The initial part of the filename the document is saved under should identify with the event. To avoid potential problems with version control further down the line, add Draft1-Date. And it is often helpful in subsequent drafts to track the changes so that people can readily see how it is evolving.

From there, you can take either of two courses: one, list the main areas to be covered under each heading in a single indented line (in other words, prepare a synopsis); or, two, copy the information and statistics from your research (but be critically selective because it is unlikely you will use it all) under the appropriate headings, along with the creative quote lines that you will have developed along the way (the notable rhetoric, but in outline form only at this stage), particularly for the introduction and conclusion. In the most appropriate spot, insert the quote, headline or announcement that defines the singular message the speech is intended to convey, the thing that above all else you want people to remember.

The singular message may be expressed as an emphatic statement in the introduction to get it into people's minds. It will be expounded in some detail in one of the key points, or be the thread that runs through them all. Without repeating it—avoiding the tell them, tell them and tell them format—you may take it a step further with a statement in the concluding section that reinforces your central objective in terms of the outcomes it is designed to achieve.

Not all speeches, though, have to be that solo-point-centric. They can canvass a broad area so long as a consistent direction is maintained throughout.

This establishes the basis for the focal point(s) directed to the audience and the principal issue and quotes that the media will pick up if it is an event worthy of media interest.

About half and half, I work from a dot point summary and from a full outline containing all the material references and quotes I intend to develop. The brief summary is generally the way to go if you are writing for someone else and you need to get approval for the synopsis before proceeding to a draft text. In that case, keep it brief. The advantage of the latter, more detailed, approach is that you begin the writing task with 2000 or more words already on paper—the speech well developed and ready to be written out, finessed and to have a bit more creative edge added in, for the logic to be put to the test and word values to be weighed up.

But it is not yet time to start writing. Otherwise you risk ending up lost in an incoherent maze of expressions that head in all directions. A few things need to be defined or cemented into your planning mindset.

Know the objective

AT THE OUTSET, BE CLEAR AS TO YOUR OBJECTIVE and how you are going to attain it. An important aspect of this is to look at where it fits in your overall communications program, or your expectations from delivering this particular speech, and what it will contribute to those objectives. This is what I mean by saying a speech should be viewed as integral to the total communication effort. Keep firing questions at it to establish the purpose and direction of the exercise. Why are you there? What is your role?

What does the organisation, or the individual speaker, get out of it? What is in the timing? Is this the kickstart to a PR or ad campaign? Is it to support one already under way? Is it a positioning opportunity to profile the organisation in the media and public perceptions? Is it to launch a new product or service or to make an announcement of moment? Is it an exercise in issues management?—say, related to environmental contamination, what is being done to resolve it, to indicate whether people directly affected need to take special precautions and what their involvement is to be, and to explain the communication plan you are putting in place to keep them informed. Is customer relations the priority? Do you want governments to get your message? Is this the genesis of something you hope to become a popular movement? Is it to generate public support, and possibly to secure government grants and corporate and private sponsorship, for a worthy cause such as research into an increasingly prevalent terminal illness or a beneficial community project? And so on.

In a large organisation, the speechwriter will be dealing with a wide range of people, often with differing interests. There are the speaker, the people running the event from within or liaising with external organisations over it, the program co-ordinators, people assigned to research support, and other areas of the organisation that have a genuine influence or want to exert their presence. To manage them for the result you want, take care, but take no prisoners.

Set the fundamental objective, agenda and direction of the speech with the speaker and the person who is working closely with the speaker and will be your principal point of liaison throughout the exercise.

There will be times as it nears the final draft where you need the mettle to stick to your plan and be prepared to convince others to do likewise to avoid the primary objective being subverted. The speakers themselves at times change tack with the prevailing breeze, generally as a consequence of whoever has been in their ear of late; at other times in accord with their constantly changing view of the corporate direction. Other areas of the organisation will endeavour to assert their interests. Sometimes they will come up with a valid point. But in the main, no; out of self-interest, their objective will be to needle their way in to promote their niche in the business. And they can be difficult to dissuade without the relationship becoming somewhat acrimonious. The courage of your conviction and your persuasiveness need to come into play, as diplomatically as you can apply them, to move these conflicting currents into the flow of the mainstream—the tide that captured at the flood leads to fortune, or, in this case, a rhetorical masterpiece.

Events outside the writer's control may force changes to the speech or the way it is managed on the day. Almost as if it was predestined, companies have a habit of dropping a clanger in an announcement to the stock exchange the day before a keynote speech is scheduled. Anti-groups have an uncanny sense of timing in coming out with damaging statements that make the last kind of headlines you want and this can have a significant influence on the media's approach. The media covering the event will come with the most apparent viewpoint in mind—the criticism or expectation created by pre-publicity or an alert from an outside source. They will have gathered all the opposing points of view from the activist groups and your competitors. This will form the agenda in effect, and they will be looking to the speaker to counter the criticism. But that need not direct the course of the speech. Often, as the saying goes, attack is the best means of defence. The best approach generally is to present more compelling argument and imagery that effectively dismiss the preconceived negative case and recapture the agenda.

Where there are controversial issues involved, opposing forces tend to adopt one of two very effective strategies: one, anticipate the case you are going to make and produce the evidence, real or contrived, to undermine it; or, two, create unrealistic expectations around what you are going to expound. The international climate change conference held in Australia in January 2006 illustrates the second method of attack. The Federal Opposition and Green movement upped the ante by arguing in advance that the conference would be meaningless unless it set specific targets for reduced greenhouse gas emissions, which clearly it was not going to do. The Greens and alternative energy groups fired a second salvo claiming the conference was a set-up to support the coal industry and foster increased tolerance of nuclear power generation. A damaging, and at times not even directly related, media report also has propensity to subvert a carefully planned agenda.

The shot across the bow can also come from within. I wrote a speech for an executive in the second tier of management to deliver to an international conference, signalling the company's long-term global intentions as a positive move, although it acknowledged there were difficulties in gaining access to the particular sector of the overseas market. We were going to promote media coverage. The day before, the head of the company went on record bagging the restrictive regulatory regime in the market concerned as an over-riding barrier to the company's global plans. There went our media plan. We had to pretend the speech did not happen and hope nobody would notice. Fortunately, they didn't. But there is a positive side to everything—the speech was delivered, and I got paid for it.

In both business and politics, there is always a need to check the headlines and morning radio heading into the event and on the day for wild horses running loose on the street. Lead organisations need to be prepared to defend their agenda—not to react and play a game in which their critics have laid down the rules, but to reinforce their own objectives, themes, expectations and the significance of their initiative.

It is essential to be intimately aware of the viewpoints of your critics and opponents—get to know them from their public statements, from what they say to and about the organisation you are working for, monitor their web sites and chat rooms. Accept the probability you may never win them over, that there are many people on this earth whose minds are closed to all but one book. Their union with like-minded people throughout their own and other related networks strengthens their sense of right. But respect their views and show that you do, endeavour to open and maintain a genuine dialogue with them, keep them informed. Do so in the realistic expectation that they will most probably not change their public stand and that they could well use any information you provide them against you. If you stay consistently by this line, however, you will come in time to earn at least their respect, if not—just possibly—a measure of co-operation and actual engagement in what steps you are taking to allay their concerns.

Accept that there are differing points of view, but assert your belief that you are on the right path and that it will achieve the best possible outcomes. In these situations, it is not a winning option to hide, and I see little value in taking a generalised stance to present the appearance of encompassing all points of view. The combatants and the media will immediately draw the correct conclusion that you are trying to avoid being engaged in the debate. This will be perceived as evasiveness or weakness and succeed only in making your organisation a target for all the other parties.

Throughout, two simple, but noteworthy, pieces of advice hold true when any of these hurdles appear in a speechwriter's path: one, hold your nerve on the grounds of right on your side;

two, maintain your own integrity and that of the speech project. Keep these in mind as you proceed through the checklist from assignment to delivery in Chapter 10.

Stay on message

WHILE AUDIENCE RELATIONSHIPS are within our focus, let us take a look at the tendency on the part of many organisations to maintain a highly conservative, defensive stance. Accepted, a lot of people are increasingly cynical and critical of big business, though they happily pocket the dividends and capital gains, as they are of big government, though they keep demanding more of government, which must grow even bigger to meet their needs. The majority of big organisations respond by imposing the rule that it is ok to go out on the street if you must, but do not do or say anything to frighten the horses. It is my belief organisations that make a material economic and social contribution have a responsibility that extends beyond their favoured triple bottom line. It is to demonstrate leadership and engage actively in debate on the major issues facing the world, their country and their people.

There is a responsibility to apply such forthrightness in their public stance, and that should be the case when they take the stand in any public forum. Turning this to public utterances, as in delivering speeches, the thing is not to be defensive or apologetic.

Look to the strengths and advantages of the organisation, the sector you operate in, business generally, if that is your field, and how it underpins economic and social wellbeing, and what you are doing in the areas of contention such as the impact of your activities on the environment, jobs, community benefit. If it is politics, the same warm feeling of economic benefit, low interest rates, low inflation, caring for individual, family and local community preferences. But make it genuinely relate and do not overstate the claim. Essentially, you should take the high ground and give instil the necessary fibre and conviction in the message.

It is important in this context that a speech stays on message, that outside influences do not distract the key message, and the fundamental theme and key points remain intact. This is one way to keep the focus on your position and point of view in the face of criticism. It is also reinforcement of the need to know and relate to the constituency that has an interest in what you are on about—your audience.

In this respect, I would emphasise again that it is overdoing it to labour the corporate mantras or play the sales pitch. Take the approach of illustrating to the audience how what you do works to their benefit, for wider community benefit and for national benefit. What is good for Ace Enterprises is good for the country ... Often, people are also interested in how your organisation sees the future panning out, your view of the medium and longer term and what it will mean for them.

Be mindful that people want to know your perspectives and insights, your story, your experience and the lessons from it, the direction and vision that guide you. It should not be contrived therefore, but purposeful, relevant and have the speaker's imprint on it.

Just one more re-run: the message must be consistent. Look at what has been said before and has worked effectively. However, many events are repeated year after year and you should endeavour to keep the approach fresh. Resist the temptation, at least initially, to go back to last year's effort as the starting point for this year. You end up with a recurring cliché, unable to escape that mould and create something new. Plan first, plan afresh, then take a look at last year to see if there is anything that merits being incorporated or updated into the new version, or that may serve as a reference point to take this year's message a step further.

Respect your audience

RETURNING TO THE ALL-IMPORTANT NEED to respect your audience, credit them with a reasonable measure of intelligence and discernment. Avoid the print media approach where people with multiple tertiary degrees have to take a post-grad in being streetwise to communicate with the common IQ denominator of a twelve year old kid suffering a condition called disadvantage, and of TV where language is not a pre-requisite. The qualification applied to radio audiences is ownership of a mobile to be used to call up talkback with an inane comment that will have the program host (rightfully) proclaim the caller a bloody idiot and cut them off. And the media's concept of the streetwise in the main is narrowly confined to inner urban existence within a three-suburb perimeter of their CBD offices. Beyond that range, where the lives and experiences, hopes, dreams and fears of everyday people reside, the media hacks are overcome by hyperventilation as if they were on Mars.

Respect that the effort people make to come along for a speech signifies interest. Apply the planning of the speech and your creative and intellectual finesse to match and relate to that level of interest. Prepare thoroughly for the delivery so that your performance is engaging and lively. Draw confidence from the assurance that you are well prepared to rise and warm to the occasion. With such a mindset, the valium can be left safely in your pocket.

Keep it foremost in mind that while colour, imagery and inspirational ideas are important in the development of the text, people do not want anything phoney. They want a substantial message that hangs together, but their interest is also linked with a desire to get to know you. Therefore, maintain your integrity; frame it so that you talk straight, say what you mean and say it with authority.

Say it in a constructive, convincing way that persuades and informs the audience and gives them something to think about, maybe a different perspective on a theme or subject they may well be familiar with. Again, take a lesson in what not to do from the media, in which there is a strengthening trend to play up the personality and their self-opinionated stand on the issue of the day. The media has always been prominent on the public platform in shaping and leading opinion, but the traditional, relatively objective reporter and balanced commentator have long been replaced by a band of opinionated militants, the strident voices of an era of the personality cult, that resist dissent and dismiss their critics. Their views are often contrived. They are as much a threat to free speech as any other force in society. Avoid following their path.

Man, woman, persons, chairs

DO NOT HEDGE YOUR BETS by lacing the text with euphemisms. This is a big ask, I know, in an age when governments and corporates have adopted virtually a new language, debased and diffused from an intent to obfuscate and be evasive and short on definition—i.e. to establish the ability in a right of reply to say, 'Not at all, what I meant was ...' And to get away with it. No wonder the courts and legal profession do a roaring trade trying to get a handle on the imponderable nuances of our times.

They have crafted the language of the euphemism as a medium that sounds convincing, but does not mean what it says or means something entirely different. Terms like downsizing and rightsizing derive from this, along with a dictionary of corporate cultural type listings that either have no real meaning in the first place or have come into use in ways that have distorted their meaning or make them meaningless—words like culture, focus, enhance, commitment, sustainable, synergy. Neither do we *move forward* or speculate what the situation may be *at the end of the day* or a host of other equally meaningless things.

And there is correctness. Mankind is out. Supposedly it is sexist and to resort to Genesis 1:27 where 'God created man in his own image …' is more than likely to leave the imprint of a stiletto heel in the toecap of one of your new Church's brogues. In any event, I prefer humankind, and have been using the term for years. Chairman is also out irrespective that it is a generic term like mankind. I cannot find whatever it takes—some quality far more perverse than compassion or understanding—to use Chairwoman or Chairperson or, God forbid, Chair. I take the greatest care not to get into the situation of being introduced to a woman who says I'm the Chair. What can you possibly say to that? Thankfully, most of the kind wear practical, flat-soled workaday shoes.

Cultural academia is big on postmodernism. Now every era is a modern era, but what happens beyond that? Is postmodernism the state of being or non-being that follows Armageddon? It certainly doesn't sound like a life or thought cycle you would want to be caught in. Even the common reference to prehistory is a misnomer. Just ask God or Stephen Hawking.

Some euphemisms, or misnomers, can be downright offensive. Late October 2004 a news report quoted American health experts as having calculated there were 100,000 'excess deaths' in Iraq in the 18 months since the outbreak of war. Excess deaths? Excuse Me! Was it that the forces of the Coalition of the Willing (and there's a name!) were trigger happy? Or were those lately demised people considered surplus? If so, why? And by what—and whose—judgment? Let us not beat about the Bush; for the way the members of the study so demeaned human life by using that term, they should all be declared surplus and lined up against a cement wall.

The other element in this new language is the unquestioned use of catch-terms. Those prime arbiters of communication standards, the media and politicians, are the main offenders. One of the most common is to refer to people as the punters. The other is the bush, used widely and unquestioningly in Australia as a collective description of people who live outside the capitals. In fact, the demographics show that the majority of non-metropolitan residents around Australia live in urban/suburban environments in regional cities and rural towns that are the look-alikes of metropolitan suburbs. If you ask them where they are from, they will say the country—not the bush, as if it was some primitive backwoods.

Both terms are offensive. Again, it is a matter of showing understanding for your constituency and treating people with genuine interest and respect.

The use of whacko or meaningless or the latest catchy terms demeans the user and the used. People can see through it and that builds a level of cynicism and outright antagonism that can become an impenetrable barrier to genuine communication. Be fresh, clear and telling. By far the most effective approach is to tell people, this is what we believe, this is what we will do, this is how we are going to solve the problem, or to make life better.

Mastering the language

WHAT ELSE CAN YOU DO to improve your mastery of the language and deftness in its use? And then, by extension, to apply that to the task of speechwriting?

The first, and main, recommendation is to be a voracious reader of fine books—literature, history, philosophy, science and technology, and works on business practice and concepts, particularly those that draw out new ideas or define new trends in the genre of *The Landmarks of Tomorrow*, written in 1959 by Peter Drucker, *In Search of Excellence*, by Tom Peters and Robert Waterman, published 1982, Peters' latest work, *Re-imagine!*, and Dan Pink's *A Whole New Mind*. For the definitive guide to telling a story and the added benefit of being more critical of the use of words, try Robert McKee's *Story: Substance, Structure, Style, and the Principles of Screenwriting*. Read books from antiquity to the present day, but predominantly the great books from the past couple of centuries because in those is to be found the evolving language towards the way we express ourselves today—at least, should be expressing ourselves.

The advantage of reading widely in all these fields is that it builds up a background knowledge and familiarity with creative thinking and expression from which you can draw out interesting and novel links and create images. Extensive reading will give you a better feel for how a major work is structured and the possibilities to experiment with structure. It will expand your vocabulary and enable you to apply a more critical selection to the use of words. It also builds a personal knowledge bank of quotes, ideas and facts that a writer can draw upon or of which they retain sufficient recall to be able to find the detailed reference quickly.

Read speeches, contemporary and from history. Where possible, listen to speeches, in person or broadcasts of the National Press Club, the Boyer Lectures, and so on. The speeches of the current US President and British Prime Minister and the Secretary-General of the United Nations are posted on their web sites. Speeches by former political leaders are archived or linked from the web sites of their parliaments. A Net search will generally locate what the notable figures from history have said on notable occasions. Most corporations publish the speeches of their CEOs on their web sites. If your field is cultural/social, again a key word web search will find the speeches of leaders of relevant organisations. And, as with some of my suggested alternative sources of research (Chapter 7), the profiles and ideas of offbeat or futuristic thinking people can be found online in the current or archived editions of publications like Fast Company and Wired. Today the bulk of our background and keeping up to date reading can be done online, from an English language edition of the Moscow Times to the way-out news service provided by The Onion.

Accepted, these may well be stratospheric against the scope of the speech at hand. But a broad knowledge of the language and the way it has been used to good effect is a sound learning path.

Writing the spoken word

THOROUGHLY PREPARED, we come to the task of writing the text.

This is the principal test of the speechwriter—in the way the language is used and a cogent argument is developed.

Keep in mind above all else that you are writing words that will be spoken. That applies to all kinds of verbal communication in which people are working from texts or notes. With well-structured, creative use of the language and imagery, any subject can be made interesting and to reach out to people. And it should flow. Writing is generally a more elegant style of expression than the everyday speak we use, but the written word is overdone unless it can be spoken with ease.

Look for the related, but out of the ordinary, expression that will convey meaning with impact. As an example, I adapted the historical unknown great south land concept of Australia and turned it into Terror Australis in an article I wrote for an online news service around the 2002 federal election, in which the campaign centred on terror, illegal immigrants and allegations, later proved to be fabricated, of children being thrown overboard from a refugee boat in the Indian Ocean.

Getting down to the actual writing, you need to distil all the information you have assembled to the most pertinent points. Use that and your writing skill to create the images that resonate with people, draw simple analogies, make it interesting and entertaining. Where it is called for, be assertive and demonstrate that you can provide inspiration and leadership.

Some hints from experience will assist in cultivating a crisp style of writing. Don Watson says that when he was speechwriting for Keating, he would say it aloud before putting it on his screen. I find I don't need to do that—it is inherent that the words I read or write also resound—although many people may well find the practice of talking it first to be helpful. There are others who prefer to dictate what they are going to say onto a recorder and add the polish when it is put onto paper. In my modus operandi, a kind of visual/oral sense comes into play when I write. I hear the words as they appear on the screen or on paper and that makes it easy to detect any discordant note.

Simplicity encompassing dignity, meaning and effect is what we seek. Look back to the Bible for the answer. 'In the beginning God made the heaven and the earth .' (Genesis: 1–1). Ten words that tell it all and millennia later defy the sub-editor's innate urge to cut.

The challenge is to write the spoken word simply, but elegantly. That is the art of good speechwriting, of any good writing for that matter. The question is how to get to this plane, and there are a few other things I can offer that will be helpful.

The computer screen itself can be a trap. Most people can get their message over crisply when they are talking, firing off emails or writing letters to each other. But put those same people before a screen to develop a lengthy, considered document, and often they are tend to get carried away. They begin to pontificate, to write convoluted, incomprehensible sentences that run on line after line.

Try this if you find that happening—take what you have just written or the next segment you are about to do, handwrite it on a sheet of paper and then type it onto the screen. Invariably, the handwritten sentences will be simpler and shorter than the ones you have been typing. There is no scientific explanation for that. It could mean technological evolution has advanced quicker than human evolution and we are meant to write things by hand and have large rubbish bins by our desks rather than a delete key to take the cast-offs. Having practiced this method a number of times, try to apply the same discipline on the screen.

Use this technique to train yourself to write more sharply and in sentences of varied lengths. That will create a much more effective impact.

But the first challenge is simply to get down to writing. There is a condition known as the Staring Disconsolately at a Blank Page Syndrome (acronym: SDBPS---but acronyms are also overplayed in government and corporate life, and should be avoided wherever possible because no one remembers what they mean; instead, use a common description). That is why we plan so meticulously and by this time have a synopsis and ordered research material to work from. Take it point by point and get on with it. If some of the words or sentences do not sound right or need a bit more life in them, type some question marks after them and come back to sort it out later. Just get on with it. Seeing a shrink won't help because their training does not encompass this particular syndrome, and anyone who has tried to read a prescription should realise writing is not a mandatory skill in the medical profession.

Incorporate a good measure of style, flair and flamboyance, which is my way of being a bit more precise and elegant about what corporate affairs people mean when they say their executive is looking for the wow factor. Taking the concept to the extreme, one of the CEOs I wrote a keynote speech for was a tech guy, the timing was the height of the dot com boom, and he wanted to paint technology as having unlimited potential to take the world into the future. He opened the speech with a single booming word: WOW!

Links, images and humour

SPEECHES FOR THE MAIN PART are a serious matter. Except for purely social events such as weddings or birthdays, the subject is more likely to demand a cogent case built around an issue of some import than for the speaker to play the role of song and dance man/woman/person(!). The case has to be presented convincingly, which makes it a serious business. But it does not mean it has to be dry and heavy going. In fact, it will fall flat and the whole point will lose impact without plenty of imagery, life and character—the very qualities it needs for both audience interest and for the speaker to perform at their best.

One way to achieve this is by creating links or connecting two seemingly disparate facts that have come to light in the research material, or by linking two unlikely ideas or images, and extending them into a new dimension. Explained more simply, this means adding a different twist to an otherwise flat and uninteresting sequence of expression to present a new, unexpected perspective to an audience that will spark their interest and depict it to them in a new light. It is a means, to repeat the emphasis, of relating to them and their experiences and the way they see things, but also to take them that one step further. That is the difference between a point-by-point, mundane presentation and one with flair.

The humorous twist that can bring a speech to life is not of the contrived comedian hype, but derives from a deft touch of satire or irony, the ability to depict an event or series of events or an image that brings it down to earth and gets to the heart of what people are thinking, yet at the same time rises above the norm. Most people will relate to this touch. The speech, as in any human interaction, spans all walks of life. You are dealing with people who hold varied entrenched points of view, many indeed who are plainly cynical. But recognise that most see things from street level. That is not to decry prejudice or outlooks confined by narrow experience or the uncertainty of the unknown, best reflected in this era in the common reaction to the term 'globalisation'. Nor is it to denigrate the objective of the speech, which is to expand their horizons. What it will aim to do is uplift them, momentarily perhaps, and give them something to think about, momentarily perhaps. It just might be a talking point in the car on the way home, causing them to miss the drive-in sign at McDonalds, or over toast the next morning.

And make good use of anecdotes to convey the message in a personal way that accords with people. These help immeasurably to enable the audience to appreciate more clearly and understand innately what you are getting at because, done effectively, it accords with their experiences. But do try to make it a little more imaginative than the reporters who illustrate magnitude in terms of the dimensions or volume of the Melbourne Cricket Ground.

The practice of these guides will be demonstrated in the case studies and examples in the next chapter.

First, though, a brief discourse on completing the writing phase. When the going gets tough, it is not always the best option for the tough simply to get going. There are times the best way out is out. Transfix the sticking point in your mind and take a stroll out in the elements or spend an hour in the corner coffee shop. Toss some ideas around and free up the imagination to let it run loose through a field of wild ideas and phrases. Talk to yourself in your mind through the word pictures across a peripheral vision laced with satirical and ironical references through to the outrageous and sift them into a vague drift that will ultimately connect. Smile while you are walking along with the inner glow of the creative spirit. The people you pass will think you are being friendly and smile back, unaware you are a modern day Mona Lisa. But I caution against talking aloud in public or you will be had by an official looking group of hoons who will lace you in a white immobiliser jacket.

Revelations are made of these, your walk, your several coffees at the corner cafe, your undeserved certifiability. The saving grace is to take along a pen and piece of paper, and write down the key phrase that captures the descriptive image that comes to mind. It is amazing how quickly these things can slip the memory after a short lapse of time.

The critical review

In REVIEWING what you have set down, always think and look critically at the structure of your writing. You might detect a four- or five-line sentence. That can be not only difficult to comprehend, especially hearing it spoken, but will have you or your speaker gasping for breath and losing the ability to give the right emphasis to the words.

Think critically about your use of language. I will say it again that a speech should have both simplicity and elegance, and it should draw on the limits of your vocabulary and the precision of your expression.

An illustration, precisely. There is a story about Webster, who compiled Webster's dictionary, that his wife walked into the matrimonial bedroom after an evening playing bridge and found him in bed with the maid.

'Webster, I'm surprised!' cried the unsuspecting wife.

Webster is said to have displayed quite some presence of mind given the delicate, potentially explosive nature of the situation. And answered precisely, 'No, my dear, 'you are amazed. It is we who are surprised.'

Be self-critical and analytical even in small things.

Do not overdo the acknowledgments. It is enough to recognise the chairman and one or two other VIPs and use one or two generic terms to cover the principal groups of people who are present.

Avoid the tendency to state the obvious. You will have heard speakers who are hosting an event open with the line, I welcome you all here tonight. Obviously we are here and not somewhere else. Obviously it is the present, and not some other night. So why say it? I also try to get my speakers out of the common habit of ending with 'Thank you'. It is like, thank you for your perseverance, now excuse me, I will just take a much-needed sit down. The best effect a speaker can create is to pause momentarily and return with measured, triumphant step to their seat. After all, the people in the audience are the ones who should be thankful.

9. Tell it like a story

Too many speeches, especially those coming from or related to the business sector and areas like technology, are overburdened with statistics and references, acronyms and the jargon of the particular sector. Instead, think of the way some of the great dramas of history have unfolded in the telling, the story of a colourful weekend away that someone may have related in the pub on a Friday night, your favourite bedtime story, your grandparents' stories laced with endeavour and privation from earlier times. Think about how they came across and the telling features that made them dear or entertaining and real to you. Question what were the creative elements that made them so. How, despite them being narratives, did the quality of intellect came into play in the telling?

When it is put that way, storytelling sounds easy, but the reality when it comes to writing is that it is hard work, whether it is a speech, a feature article for a newspaper, a short story or a novel. But it is an art form that can be mastered within the writer's capability for conceptual, visionary thinking, their grasp of the language and the discipline of logic from which a coherent structure takes shape. I do not want to turn people off here, but it has to be appreciated that getting 90 per cent consistently on English Lit essays or being constantly praised for the quality of your presentations is not enough. To take it to a higher level, the artist is someone who not only possesses a measure of innate ability to begin with, but has a compulsive driving force of creativity that is inherent in all artistic endeavour. There are two positive, comforting elements in this. One is that that being born with the ability, these characteristics can be cultivated. In fact, they have to be cultivated and developed through dedication and intensive, consistent practice. The second is that people who are not natural born writers or speechmakers are able to reach a level of presence and presentability with practice and a rational approach—by following the planned steps I have set out and injecting their character and ideas into their speeches, whether written for someone else or themselves.

Then, with these twin elements of story and discipline, you have it—the hidden secret of being able to relate. And realise that the stories have a message and they have heart—the warmth of humanity that is overpowering for the endurance it involved, that brought you to tears, soothed you, inspired you. And there you have the essential elements of communication that transform a speech into a memorable discourse.

Story rules the conceptual age

WASHINGTON WRITER/AUTHOR, Dan Pink, has some profound wisdom to offer in this consideration of the story, which he describes as integral to the human experience. Dan and I have a connection deriving from the fact that we are both lifetime writers and opted at particular crossroads in our lives to become free agents. Dan is a onetime speechwriter to former US Vice President Al Gore, a former contributing editor to Fast Company Magazine and a contributing editor to Wired Magazine, and writes for the New York Times. More to the point in this context, he is the author of two bestsellers—*Free Agent Nation*, which for the first time defined the extent of the US population that works independently and the issues that confront them/us, and more recently *A Whole New Mind: Moving from the information age to the conceptual age*[8].

The latter work defines the six senses that dominate the emerging conceptual age as Design, Story, Symphony, Empathy, Play and Meaning. In an age when, as Dan says, facts are ubiquitous, nearly free and available at the speed of light, people continue to cling to the world of data. Why? 'Stories amuse; facts illuminate. Stories divert; facts reveal. Stories are for cover; facts are for real. The trouble with this view is twofold. First … it runs counter to how our minds actually work. Second, in the Conceptual Age, minimising the importance of story places you in professional and personal peril.' And he argues, 'What begins to matter more is the ability to place these facts in context and deliver them with emotional impact. And that is the essence of the aptitude of Story—context enriched by emotion.'[9]

Moreover, Dan asserts, stories are making significant inroads into the fact-centric world of business. Companies are giving their people lessons in storytelling, using storytelling in their knowledge management programs and creating databases of their internal stories, which arguably are of far greater value than an intranet filled with document templates, management directives and operational processes and procedures. The use of stories is also critical for businesses out in the marketplace. 'Like design, it (the story) is becoming a key way for individuals and entrepreneurs to distinguish their goods and services in a crowded marketplace.'[10]

This book is a must read to understand which way the tide of the new world is heading and how to catch it rather than drown in it—and that goes especially for writers and creative people in all fields. Check out Dan and the book at danpink.com/pink.php

The renowned authority on screenwriting, Robert McKee, asserts story is about principles, not rules. 'Anxious, inexperienced writers obey rules. Rebellious, unschooled writers break rules. Artists master the form,' McKee says in his highly instructional book, *Story*[11]. Any writer who reads *Story*—and, better still, follows it up with a number of screenplays—will emerge with a far more critical eye for context and coherence, and indeed acquire the habit of scanning every word they write with a question mark.

The Hindenburg disaster

ON 6 MAY 1937 the German zeppelin Hindenburg caught fire as it approached a mooring mast at Lakehurst Naval Air Station in New Jersey. The flames engulfed the ship within 37 seconds and 35 of the 97 people aboard were killed, along with a member of the ground crew. It goes without saying this was big news at the time, but what made it especially notable was the graphic recorded radio eyewitness report of American journalist, Herbert Morrison, which became one of the most famous broadcasts in history.

Contrast the raw emotion at the horror of this scene in Morrison's account with the generally more dispassionate reports of disasters around the world today, which almost invariably generate as much feeling and empathy as sitting in a laundromat:

It burst into flames! ... It's burning and it's crashing! It's crashing, terrible! Oh, my! Get out of the way, please! It's burning, bursting into flames and is falling on the mooring mast, and all the folks between ... oh, this is terrible. This is one of the worst catastrophes in the world! It's a terrific

115

crash, ladies and gentlemen, it's smoke and it's flames,
now, and the frame is crashing to the ground, not quite to
the mooring mast ... Oh, the humanity, and all the
passengers screaming around here.

The case studies I have included cover a varied range of
speechwriting assignments from my experience as Victorian
Premier Jeff Kennett's chief speechwriter and subsequently as
keynote speechwriter to a number of leading Australians in various
fields. They illustrate some of the different approaches that can be
taken and the points I have been making throughout this and the
preceding chapters—how to create the connections and images, to
write with a measure of style, to tailor a speech to the interests of a
particular audience, and mould the messages in a way that captures
people's attention.

One-up for the messenger

ON AN AUTUMN DAY in 1993, within six months of his election,
Victorian Premier Jeff Kennett was heading out of Melbourne in
his official car, VIC 1—a miniature State flag flapping on the front
of the bonnet, a quirk of his—to address the graduation ceremony
at Ballarat University College. The headline in his speech was an
announcement that at the end of the year Ballarat would be
granted full university status. This was one of his early moves to

fete the state's main regional cities where some eight marginal seats would one day decide his fate.

I am sitting—at ease with him on the road—at a makeshift desk in the rapidly expanding media office in the Premier's Private Office, Level 1, 1 Treasury Place. The phone rings with a familiar insistent tone.

'Quill, what the hell's this?'

He had been doing the usual last-minute, cursory pre-read of the speech and reached page two. The notes there reflected on his inglorious academic background, something he readily acknowledged publicly, and I had picked it up for a bit of fun. The story he told of his sole year at the Australian National University was that it ended with he and the examiners differing over what was a pass mark. The speech repeated the story, but added a punchline, 'In fact, I remember year nine at high school as the best three years of my life.'

Historical connections

FORMER TELSTRA CEO, Dr Ziggy Switkowski, and his close advisers always ensured he went well-prepared on any key speaking engagement and that the speech struck the right tone for the occasion. This was a task that often came my way, working with his chief of staff and head of media and communications. With his address for the 80th anniversary of Telstra Research Laboratories, the core message was TRL's voyage of discovery from the pioneering days of telecommunications.

Part of the way we sought to push this message home was by connecting the historical links, and they came from the background research I had done. It pointed out that TRL was established fewer than 50 years after the invention of the telephone, the same year wireless telegraphy was first used for a broadcast in Australia and that the country's first regular radio station went to air, the year the first sod was turned for the construction of Canberra—relevant given the Federal Minister was present—and that TRL's foundation in 1923 preceded the establishment of Australia's great national research institution, CSIRO, by three years.

Taking it a step further, the research uncovered the combination of two significant, seemingly unrelated events in TRL's founding year. This was the year John Logie Baird invented television and, in the US, Clarence Birdseye invented frozen food. But by putting them together—television and the advent of fast food—we drew a light-hearted reference to these discoveries as the origin of what, some 40 years on, would become the era of the couch potato.

Much the same approach was adopted for a short speech at a ceremony where Telstra made a large donation to the Peter MacCallum Cancer Centre in Melbourne for a new program to treat adolescent sufferers. The Telstra sponsorship and corporate affairs people sent me the event program and a sales line—in effect, what a great and benevolent company we are.

But online research pointed me to the story of Sir Peter MacCallum, the centre's co-founder. He left school aged 12, determined though that he should continue his education, and worked to put himself through school and university. For decades from the 1920s he was an Australian leader in the field of radiology and a leading advocate for cancer research and treatment. Coincidentally, the institution named after him was established around the time the first chemotherapy drugs came into use in the late 1940s. Here was an amazing story, with a very human touch, for a speech like this. It comes together when you add the link that today Peter Mac, as it is known, is continuing in that pioneering spirit and has become one of the world's renowned cancer research and treatment centres.

Courage under fire

THEN DR SWITKOWSKI delivered the annual Town and Gown Dinner lecture at Melbourne University in 2001, we built the centrepiece around Australia as a smart country and our future prospects within that concept.

We drew on history and used that to look into the future. The speech contained the line, 'We all, to my mind, need a dose of courage under fire—in effect, the courage to cast a futuristic vision, and then to meet the challenges it presents.'

The term, 'courage under fire', was used deliberately because the majority of people would have been familiar with it from either or both of two sources—the popular movie of that name that came out in 1996, and an unbeaten horse called Courage Under Fire who was the star of the Australasian harness racing world at the time. These images can come from all sorts of strange places. The thing is that people can connect with them.

We used a background historical reference to lead into a dissertation on the future of technology. Having done my homework by reading the previous half-dozen Town and Gown lectures on the Net, we were able to contrast Dr Switkowski's approach with them by indicating that while previous speakers drew on history for their themes, we would be looking into the future. Here are the introductory lines:

We all warm to the allure of a sunburnt country, as Dorothea Mackellar described it—even though it might not be evident from Melbourne's weather at the moment. Author Marcus Clarke may have appreciated it better from an early European perspective when he wrote, 'Australia has rightly been named the Land of the Dawning ... In Australia alone is to be found the grotesque, the weird, the strange scribblings of nature learning how to write.'

Today we are establishing new concepts of civilisation and developing the tools that enable us to take our place in a global world. The legends and unique nature of the bush remain in our hearts, but the new world is built on knowledge. It is something to which we are beginning to come to terms, but a long, demanding road lies ahead. Knowledge, especially in the field of science, does not stand still and leave us with the opportunity to catch up: we have to lead the way in a field that really has become a fourth dimension alongside the financial, community and environmental elements of the triple bottom line.

Many of my predecessors at the Town and Gown over the years have inevitably looked to history for inspiration. I intend to contrast that by looking to the future—the aspirations we hold, the imperatives and challenges we face, and what we must do to meet them.

This therefore is ideally the forum in which we should seek to unmask the question of how Australia becomes a smart country.

One more from Dr Switkowski, this time addressing the 2004 Australia Business Arts Foundation Awards, an example of how to link your organisation to the host organisation and its objectives:

At Telstra, we talk a lot about the value of our communications technology in keeping Australians connected and making a positive contribution to their lifestyles. In similar vein, the Foundation is an invaluable point of connect between business, the arts and the community. Telstra is one of the nation's largest supporters of the arts. This is not simply a matter of largesse—that would be a highly dubious motive—but an abiding commitment to partner in the work of arts organisations and support the community that we serve.

The mother of all hangovers

BACK TO JEFF KENNETT, and in the Menzies Lecture delivered in Canberra in August 1995 he spoke of a country that was heading towards a new century but had lost the spirit of its founders.

The lecture exhorted people to look once more to the future. It warned, in a typically Australian reference and one that had the overtone of a comment Saddam Hussein made at the onset of Gulf War I: 'The risk, if we continue this way, is that we will all wake up on January 1, year 2001, with the mother of all hangovers, but nothing will have changed.'

The lecture was given more media coverage than any other political speech that year, and I noted with some pride two days later that it was lauded in the lead editorial in the Melbourne Herald Sun under the heading, 'The father of a lecture.'

Looking beyond the borders

KENNETT, rather than a federal politician or a business leader, was invited to deliver the inaugural Pacific Partnership Lecture to the Australian American Leadership Dialogue Forum in 1997. His national standing and constant hectoring on the need to come to terms with a borderless world were the most probable reasons.

The setting was the spacious ballroom at Raheen in the plush eastern Melbourne suburb of Kew, the former palace of Catholic archbishops and now—$35 million worth of renovations later—of billionaire cardboard king Dick Pratt. There, Kennett sought to assert Australia's unique characteristics and position, to draw the obvious comparisons with America, and emphasise what he called a global civic responsibility vested in tandem in each country.

This was an impressive gathering of some 70 political, business and media figures from the two countries. It included the Washington bureau chief of the New York Times, Johnny Apple (although with a name like that, I wondered why he had moved to Washington), Washington Post columnist, E.J. Dionne, wife of former Australian Coalition leader, Carolyn Hewson, and businesswoman, Janet Holmes a Court.

The speech was Clintonesque and the Americans saw it in the light of their land of hope and glory. The Australians, like Federal Minister Simon Crean and wife Carole sitting at my table, were a little less enthusiastic, wanting something more domestic. I pondered the possibility that the tyranny of distance remains embedded in Australian minds.

For the Americans, the thank you toast to the Premier was proposed by the soon to be Deputy Secretary of State, Richard Armitage, a man square in physique from the head down, the veteran of three combat tours with the US Navy in Vietnam, father of eight children. Armitage has the kind of presence that if he barked an order at you to go torch a village, you would do it for God and country, and because it would take a lot more courage to defy a man of his demeanour than torch a village. He talked of US–Australian relations being forged on the world's battlefields and ended with a quote from a poem called 'The Peaceful Warrior', which I do not recall him mentioning in his Deputy Secretary's role during the early phase of the latter Iraq war.

I might mention as an indulgent aside that I always come away from events like this—events of some moment, the grand setting, the people of note, the sense of privilege at having been present—and write a personal account as my memoir of it, but usually with the satirical edge from which this description has been drawn.

Observe in this case that the historical background provides the link into an assessment of the situation at the time and the future vision. You will also see repeated reference to this part of the world as Asia Pacific. At my instigation, we adopted this description in place of the more commonly used term, the Asia Pacific region. The reason—Australia's geographic sphere is more than the limited confine that the term region connotes, rather a hemisphere of countries that are increasingly coming and working together, with cross-cultural links, and of growing global importance. In fact, to give it added impact I turned the world on its side and sometimes termed the region the Asia Pacific hemisphere.

Kennett opened his lecture:

We and our ancestors have trodden many paths to Australia. People have been forced to come to Australia to acquit their debt to society, incited here by the adventure of discovery, driven here by adversity in their own homelands, and subsequently lured here by the scent of opportunity and the ideal of freedom … We are accordingly a mixed culture that has long been the all important southern outpost of the Pacific.

Suddenly we are in the midst of a region about to dominate world economic growth and cultural change for perhaps some hundreds of years … Australia's future— unique among all the countries of the world—is here in the vast bowl of the Pacific where we are able to bridge the cultures and economies between the East and West. We occupy an all important satellite footprint that keeps the Pacific trading post open while the rest of the world sleeps.

Then the link to America:

Our futures—those of Australia and America—are inextricably bound in the cauldron of Asia Pacific. We come with some similar perspectives to this point in what I regard very positively as a maturing relationship. Australia, despite its much smaller size, presents a great opportunity for America as a broker in Asia Pacific …

There are distinguishing likenesses in the spirit of our countries. In our two nations the fires of freedom and democracy burn fiercely. We are inspired by the strength of an innate independence, and committed to fairness and opportunity as rights. From our tandem experiences at building new Western civilisations, remote at the time from the rest of the world, we have hewn these values. Australians and Americans have fought and died to preserve them, and protected an often fragile peace in troubled places around the world.

Then, looking to the future and the need for the information age to confer equal benefit:

Our generation is managing and shaping a period of transition for generations that will inherit a new world … We must look to the principles that create and support strong, thriving societies in an interconnected world. The information age has changed, and will continue to change, the world for the better. Through this major advance, the template for a new era has been cast in the past 16 years. We are nurturing a generation who have no direct experience of the events that have marked the history of the 20th century, but to whom electronics is second nature. For them, there must be a balance between technological advances and civic values in order to optimise the benefits of these advances for the wider community.

Finally, the social obligation to the world that rests with America, prescient to some extent as to the deteriorating world view of America in the new century in the wake of September 11 and the pounding of Iraq:

The overwhelming dominance of the United States in technology and its global influence in this era will be far greater than it ever was in the Cold War, and it would be easy to be complacent in such circumstances. America needs to determine how it will handle the social impact of its position, and to consider it as a global civic responsibility. It must be remembered a lot of people already resent America's world influence. The issues are how is America going to manage its social agenda globally? and how are others going to react to its position? Certainly in this region we would not like to see a repeat of the situation depicted in the 1950s book, 'The Ugly American'"[1].

Telling it to the world

THE THEME of the Pacific Partnership Lecture flowed through into Kennett's keynote address to the World Economic Forum in Hong Kong later in 1997. Again he drew on the strengths of Australia's multicultural make-up in a changing world:

Australians ... have learned how to live together ... whatever our country of origin, as we identify with greater certainty our place in the world. The tolerance of Australians, the harmonious nature of our society and its richly diverse culture today provide the potential for Australia to play an important partnership role together with the other countries in Asia Pacific as we all strive for growth in a global world ... In size, however, we cannot be considered a major global force in our own right, and must seek to draw strength and exert what influence we can through forging strategic alliances and partnerships ... Our strengths ... will be marshalled to the task of advancing the growth of the Asia Pacific hemisphere.

Taking a constitutional

THE REPUBLICAN DEBATE of 1998--99 was inflated by so much hot air and diverted by so much devious politicking that any thought of changing the Constitution was bound to float out of sight. The Constitutional Convention of February 1998 was typical except for a single incisive contribution.

Tom Burton described it in an opinion column in the Australian Financial Review: 'The contrast could not have been clearer. Victorian Premier Jeff Kennett flew into Canberra on Wednesday morning for his only appearance at the Constitutional Convention. In a 10-minute speech he showed more leadership and purpose than the Prime Minister (John Howard) did in two weeks of jesuitical fence-sitting. Kennett's timing was perfect. With the republican camp deeply divided, his simple and logical speech in support of a president appointed by two-thirds of all federal MPs caught the mood of the convention.'

Here's a sample of what Kennett, the former avowed monarchist turned pro-republican, had to say in strongly instructive fashion: 'If we are going to make the change ... it must be with honour and deep gratitude for what the connection to the monarchy has meant throughout the period of Australian settlement in terms of the basic institutions of Australian democracy … There is no justifiable proposal that we abandon our system of responsible government within a parliamentary democracy …'

Of his proposal for the election of a president: 'An election structured in this way delivers both a republic and importantly an improvement on the present position. It requires the Prime Minister and Opposition leader to agree on the appointment and in this way would blow a refreshing wind of consent through the corridors of our Westminster system.'

Preamble for the new millennium

IN APRIL 1999, at the height of the republican debate leading to the referendum that towards the end of the year was soundly defeated, Kennett assigned me to write a new Preamble to the Australian Constitution. It was in response to Prime Minister Howard's suggested Preamble, a fairly pedestrian and much derided effort written for him by the poet Les Murray. The PM had faxed it around the State and Territory leaders for their feedback.

The research and writing of Kennett's Preamble, that we entitled Declaration of the People of Australia so as to be a statement of intent on the part of the people, took 64 hours over the course of about a week and a half—one hour for every two of the 128 words, deliberately producing a version much shorter Howard's 169 words.

The research examined some of the major declarations of national and individual identity throughout history and their philosophical links, of which all but the Magna Carta basically derive from the philosophy of John Locke, especially the notion of a Contract of Society as outlined in his Two Treatises of Government of 1690. Locke's contention that it is held to be self-evident that all persons are created equal and endowed with inalienable rights is the central thread through the other declarations of rights and constitutions that were canvassed as part of this exercise. They are the State of Virginia Declaration of Rights of 12 June 1776, the United States Declaration of Independence of 4 July 1776, the United States Constitution which came into effect on 4 March 1789, the French Declaration of the Rights of Man and the Citizen of July/August 1789, and President Abraham Lincoln's address at Gettysburg cemetery of 19 November 1863, in which he referred to the creation of 'a new nation, conceived in Liberty, and dedicated to the proposition that all men are created equal', and provided a vision of 'a new birth of freedom—and that government of the people, by the people, for the people, shall not perish from the earth.'

Research material at hand, the second major step was to establish the objectives and concept of our statement. It was to draw on the Australian heritage, character and diversity but, in a sense, in the abstract—to imply the nature of Australianism without having to set out detailed events or characteristics in a way so as not to be static, but futuristic. It had to inspire and to last. Last, as Kennett said on radio, for 3000 years!

The State Treasurer Alan Stockdale vehemently challenged its reference that 'We hold inviolable the rights of a free people.' Stockdale insisted the word should be 'inviolate'. At a meeting with Kennett and Stockdale, I stood my ground, arguing inviolable is not (or never) to be violated, whereas inviolate simply means not violated (in the present time). And won the day.

Coverage the morning after it was released and widely circulated to leaders around the country was extensive and positive, especially in the Melbourne Herald Sun, which devoted its front page to 'Kennett's vision for the nation' under a banner headline, 'MY WAY', and a photograph of the Premier with a print of the declaration inserted beside him. The Age used graphics to illustrate the main historical influences. The Australian presented it as a challenge to the Prime Minister—as indeed all the papers had noted, the key references to God and mateship from the Howard Preamble were missing from Kennett's. Under a 'Presidential Jeff' headline, The Australian newspaper's columnist, Frank Devine, took the opportunity to look at the Premier's national influence.

I maintain it to be a statement worthy of Australia and Australians and of the test of time, and place the full text of the Declaration of the People of Australia on the record in the hope it will be given earnest consideration the next time we vote not to be a republic:

The Constitution of Australia

DECLARATION OF THE PEOPLE OF AUSTRALIA:

We commit ourselves to the Commonwealth of Australia as a sovereignty founded on the values of equality and dignity.

We hold inviolable the rights of a free people—to speak freely and make our own choices in the pursuit of knowledge, opportunity and fulfilment.

Australia's distinctive identity and lifestyle are to be prized and cherished.

We celebrate difference, and are united by the heritage of a harmonious indigenous and international culture, and the custodianship of an ancient, fragile land.

The future is our frontier and our destiny is to claim Australia's place in the world.

Our democracy is vested in every individual and confers the protection of the rule of law; and government serves the common good.

In this spirit the Constitution defines Australia's charter for all generations.

14 April 1999

Aces are trumps

AND WE COME TO my first serious foray into the sporting world. Now, I grew up around racing stables, and horse racing (and losing money on it) has always been my sporting passion, but this was one right out of the box—from the glamour court of world women's tennis.

It came early 2005 and was the right prescription to end what felt at the time like an interminable losing streak on the nags and add some spice to my life. I was commissioned in the middle of the second week of the Australian Open to write a speech for what would be the rising Australian star Alicia Molik's first public appearance following the Open—the launch of a national education program on organ and tissue donation and transplantation, with students from the senior years at Melbourne High School as the audience. I landed the job through the national organ donor co-ordinating body, Australians Donate, as a consequence of having been regular speechwriter for its chairman, Marcia Coleman, since 2003. They secured Alicia for half an hour to head the launch; Alicia needed a speech. The network came good and I was in the right place at the right time.

What a much-needed tonic! My brother had been in a hospital intensive care unit since before Christmas, the computer virtually executed itself on the eve of New Year's Eve and took three days to get back to working order, I had been through a few lean months and was broke and seizing upon every bit of work I could get, and another holiday season was coming to an end with no holiday. A late afternoon call put me in the frame of mind that I recalled as a toddler going to the beach for the first time, at once excited and in awe, only this time I did not run away in fright.

Next day, Australia Day, was the day before Alicia's 24th birthday, the day that as one of the first Australians (along with Lleyton Hewitt) to make the quarter-finals of the Open in 17 years, she played the match of her life to be beaten narrowly and unluckily on line calls by the world's No.1, Lindsay Davenport. Two days later she teamed with Russian Svetlana Kuznetsova to win the doubles, her first grand slam title and ironically against a pair headed by Davenport.

How to approach it—dealing with a young woman short of half my age, an audience of teenage students (and inevitably a media pack), and a subject that centres on life and death, mostly death, and scares most people, when Alicia's presence and the still very vivid images of the Open will have tennis on everyone's mind?

I read the newspaper reports, her quotes, listened to her TV interviews, and built up the impression of someone who talks fast in youthful fashion, who is very natural and confident in her approach, yet thinks fast and responds accordingly, just like in her tennis.

Her theme, or motto, as I read, was 'Don't die wondering.' That could well have gone down like a lead balloon at a launch on organ donation, that is until you appreciate that she applies it in a spirit of personal commitment and goes all out for it—prepared, but not afraid, to lose. Then it becomes relevant and can be used to advantage to meet her needs and connect her to this young audience. This, then, is how we sailed into what by then were known waters, well prepared—and by this time feeling less than half our age:

The past two weeks I've just had the best time of my life—playing the centenary Australian Open and taking it further than I've ever done in a grand slam before.

It's been the greatest feeling to achieve this in my home country and I could feel the support that was there for me, knowing in the back of my mind that most of Australia was looking on, and that they were all in my corner.

I don't need to tell you that tennis is my life's commitment. It gives me so much to fill my life and I get so much out of playing the game at the highest level.

Taking up this theme, we all need to have a commitment to life. And that's what the education program on organ and tissue donation is about—to be committed to grow in awareness and compassion for the needs of other Australians.

Organ donation is pretty much a touchy subject and a lot of people feel uncomfortable with it, but it shouldn't scare you.

I approach my life generally and my tennis with the motto, "Don't die wondering." It means that I go for it and I don't step away from a challenge.

Australia Day—the day before my birthday—was a historic day in 17 years for Australians, since 1988, at our own grand slam tournament. I lost, but I'm not regretting it for a minute because I played the best tennis in my career against the Number One in the world—I went for it, and I wasn't afraid to lose.

Winning the doubles two days later, and against Linsday Davenport, for my first grand slam title really put the icing on my birthday cake.

Now I'm committed to going on from there.

Grand slam tennis means walking into the spotlight of world attention and putting your ability on the line against an opponent who wants to blast you off the court. You don't think of it as being scary—you can't afford to or you'd never make it onto centre court.

And the issue of organ donation is challenging, but we need to understand and face it and come to know that we can do something very positive about it …

I really think it's important for you to consider this as part of your education, leading to accepting responsibility for the way you live and for the welfare of other people. You are taught healthy lifestyle, to eat well, play sport, play tennis. We're just talking about organ donation as another aspect of this approach.

Oscar nominations

THE QUESTION is bound to arise: out of all the things I have written, what ranks as the best?

There are three nominations, and each could take the award. One is the suggested Preamble to the Australian Constitution (Chapter 8) written for Premier Jeff Kennett—for the intensity of the assignment, the end result (a satisfying achievement of the seemingly impossible) and its wide impact.

The second was Michael Roux's welcoming address as chairman of the Australian Davos Connection for an international leadership retreat at which the audience comprised most of the influential figures in Australia and leaders worldwide in politics, business, the arts and science and technology. The retreat was held in very recent times, but the date, venue and participants cannot be mentioned because the tentacles of security reach even into my world.

The assignment began with a brief interview in which I found myself warming to a like-minded thinker. We discussed the need to exhort this leadership group to put the major issues of a troubled world on the mainstream agenda and go out into the world using their influence to make a difference. The way we would do this would be not only to highlight the principal issues, but illustrate the potential direction of leadership to them through such examples. These were to be Aristotle's concept of the 'good society', Martin Luther King Jr's famed letter on injustice that he penned in Birmingham Prison, and people's capacity for greatness as personified in the life of M.K. Gandhi.

Michael was scheduled to talk for ten minutes; the text of the initial draft ran close to twenty. I cut it back to size, but Michael liked the first full draft so much that he went with it. Some extracts from the introduction:

> I draw a parallel to what the noted physicist, Professor Stephen Hawking, has posed as the quest for 'the ultimate triumph of human reason'. His view on the direction of science mirrors the guidelines for our Retreat. It is that, '…most scientists have been too occupied with the development of new theories that describe *what* the universe is to ask the question *why*.'
> But to that should be added a further question—*why not?*— to establish the full perspective of what it is desirable for us to draw from our discussions. Then we have the basis to arrive at the main objective of our agenda, which is to *make a difference.*

Almost two-and-a-half millennia after Aristotle and Plato, one of our principal endeavours remains adhered to their belief that we need to learn to live together productively and peacefully.

The ultimate reference point of the Aristotelian notion of the 'good society' is the overall good of the community rather than individual welfare—although our experience is that the good of the community translates into individual benefit. His concept finds a modern expression in the social contracts of governments and the social responsibility of business.

That illustrates the timelessness of incontrovertible principles that reach to the soul of human matter ... It has to do with injustice and disregard for dignity, which should smite our consciences no matter where injustice, oppression and suffering occur in the world. As Martin Luther King Junior asserted in his famed letter from Birmingham Prison, 'I am here because injustice is here ... Injustice anywhere is a threat to justice everywhere. We are caught in an inescapable network of mutuality, tied in a single garment of destiny.'

We find ourselves in the sardonic position of trying to live up to the ideals that history has shown us are within the realm of capability while we are mired in conflict, inhumanity and an ethos of frustration and rebellion.

How, in these circumstances, do we find a meaningful way? In essence, it is to look within ourselves, and may well lie within the sentiment of the lawyer in Harper Lee's *To Kill a Mockingbird*, 'The one thing that doesn't abide by majority rule is a person's conscience.'

We moved on to challenges facing Australians, young and ageing, and for Australia's place in the world:

For Australians, one of the most important issues is that we are in something of a hiatus in which there is widespread confusion, especially among younger Australians, about our identity, and consequently about where we stand in the region and the world.

Our young people today are going to Gallipoli to find the roots of their identity. We need to equip them to come to terms with a different sense of meaning that will give them a vision of Australia. From Terra Australis Incognita—to what? We have to help them answer this question to paint a realistic picture of the future.

A critical future challenge lies in our changing demographic profile. This has not yet been debated to the point of any effective conclusion and there is need for an economy-wide focus on how to cater for an ageing population and its impact on the nation as a whole.

We're undergoing a shift in Australia's position. How do we see it and take advantage of it? What are the pressures we'll come under in future years as the world itself changes?

To elicit some meaningful answers, these questions are posed in confronting terms within our agenda—are we to become the 23rd province of China or the 52nd state of America? And among the key relationships within the region, Australia's links with China and Japan create a tense and not so equal triumvirate.

And drawing this to a conclusion:

Gandhi believed that our greatness as human beings lies not so much in being able to remake the world, as in being able to remake ourselves—or, to express that in one of his most memorable quotes, 'You must be the change you wish to see in the world.'

But in reality the challenge before us … is a combination of those two concepts. It is to gain a deeper understanding of our world, to accept the constraints to the personal assumptions that we hold and appreciate that there are diverse views on which the consensus is much broader than our own perceptions.

If we were to accept the situation around the world at face value, we'd be overwhelmed because there is so much that we could be depressed about. But we need to take control and gain a sense of purpose, and then to realise that each of us can have an influence.

… Aristotle … was every bit a modern day person in his thinking about the way we live together. After all this time, our advancement remains a work in progress. We are surrounded by false prophets, our fragility under pressure leads us to shift values all too easily, as demonstrated by the reaction to terror.

What I have painted as the canvas against which this Retreat is being held can be summed up best, I think, in the expression of Martin Luther King Junior: 'Human progress never rolls on wheels of inevitability … We must use time creatively, in the knowledge that the time is always ripe to do right.'

The third nomination is one I wrote and delivered myself to a church full of family and friends in the north-western Melbourne suburb of Keilor in May 2005—a eulogy to my brother, Bill, who died in hospital from a respiratory problem. Bill, it should be explained, was born with severe cerebral palsy, unable to feed himself or talk or make much use of his hands, and was wheelchair-bound for much of his almost 56 years on this earth.

We went through a day and night bedside vigil followed by a day making funeral arrangements and letting everyone concerned know of his death, some 45 hours without sleep. When a sense of reality returned after the overwhelming emotion of that time, I accepted that as the senior surviving family member I should be the one to deliver the eulogy. But more than that, I wanted to. I could have carried the intense emotion of the experience of his death into the church but knew had I done that, I would have had the most extreme difficulty in holding it together, and it would have caused distress to the people at the service. Therefore, in writing and preparing for the eulogy, I raised it a level to reach out to his immediate and extended family—the many people who had been involved in his care and those with disabilities like his own who had shared his life—and depicted it as a celebration of his life with the title, 'Our Brother Bill.' A summary in extracts:

> In the course of Thursday, when Bill was admitted to hospital, there were times his little cubicle was crowded with people. Our family was there, along with a crew from SCOPE (the former Spastic Society of Victoria). And there were many, many other people who were thinking of us, and with us in spirit. I observed at one point that it was like a family reunion as Bill fought to hold the final remnant of his rich life and be part of it.
>
> I reflect on that because I want you to regard our get-together as a reunion of Bill's family. We are all his family—those of us who are directly related, and his wider, extended family in the Keilor and St Albans area. It must

be remembered, after all, that he spent almost half his life here. This was his home and his life.

Above all, this reunion is to set aside our remorse and to celebrate the life of Bill …

The singular thing about Bill from his earliest years was an indomitable spirit that enabled him to surmount what might have seemed at first appearance to be impossible barriers. He was born trapped in a body that basically didn't work except for the extraordinary dexterity he exercised with his feet. Yet he was possessed of one of the sharpest minds imaginable and an iron will such that he accepted no handicap.

A few things typify (his life) … One was the Friday pub nights to sink a few beers and have a counter tea with his mates from Milas Court (his community house). He had a keen appreciation for pretty girls. And being a farm boy originally, he loved animals. But since one of the family's more tenuous and riskier occupations involved the training and riding of jumps horses, racing and having an occasional bet were second nature to him. In short, he was steeped in pretty well all the traditional wholesome Australian vices …

Bill's eye for colour in his choice of clothes reflects something far deeper—an innate creativity (which) found its most profound expression in painting despite that it was a painstaking process for him to produce pictures holding the brushes between his toes. The breadth of his understanding of human nature, even of himself, of being able to depict character, moods and images on canvas has to be seen to be believed …

The enormous strength and courage and the independence and sense of adventure that characterised him are things we could all do well to take to heart.

Bill's life as a whole was an undeniable affirmation of the endurance of the human spirit—the will not just to survive, but to prevail. This is the spirit that we loved so much in him, that is now free of the difficulties he had to live with and free at last of suffering, the spirit of Bill that remains a part of all of us.

In Nomine Domini—In the Name of God.

Bill's half life-size self-portrait, capturing his character and mannerism to perfection, hangs in my lounge as an enduring memorial that says far more than those words. But as I found over the following months, the words themselves circulated around the family as if they had become some form of gospel.

10. Ready, aim, deliver

Firm guidelines and timelines for commissioning speeches and getting them finalised are essential. The writer and the team they are working with should initially set out a workable process that takes account of the time to set out the initial assignment, do the research, plan it, write it, develop the graphics and get it approved, then all-importantly for the speaker to get a handle on what they are going to say.

This chapter details the timelines—what needs to be done and when—and how to approach the assignment, and the most effective ways to prepare for and perform the delivery.

Setting deadlines

1. **Set a firm sequence of deadlines:**

   i.   To get the background to the writer, and undertake any additional research or interviews that may be required;

   ii. To prepare a synopsis and secure approval for the general approach;

   iii. To develop a first draft;

   iv. To get that back to the people managing the event for their additional input—that is, your own event co-ordinators, or in many cases it will be the person in your organisation who is the point of liaison for the external organisation running the event;

   v.   To get it to the speaker for further direction from them;

   vi. To canvass it with people who will provide direction towards the final draft, and MDs and executives from any of the business divisions that may have an interest in that they or their activities are rating a mention;

   vii. To enable the identification of potential media opportunities, including the option of adding in an announcement that will make news;

viii. To enable the preparation, where appropriate, of briefing notes on related issues, and Q&As for the speaker;

ix. To allow adequate time to prepare the speaker for the event;

x. In the case of someone writing their own speech, allow yourself ample time to become fully familiar with it, which will give you greater comfort in approaching the delivery, but do not let the luxury of time and the opportunity to read and re-read allow doubts to emerge. If that happens, you will rewrite instead of re-read. Correct things that may be wrong and change things that do not seem to make sense, but do not get into a panic and start rewriting the whole thing. You have followed the planning and development process; it will be ok. Much better to get your attitude pointed the right way.

2. Arrangements for graphics:

Liaise through the main organisational contact with the graphics designers who will put the pack of slides together where it is required or desired. Most corporate organisations and governments will use master slide templates that have their logos embedded in them. They also have people who are good at developing graphics and even, where appropriate, adding sound effects.

But they need guidelines, and where you know slides are needed it is the best idea to headline and number them within the text upon completion of the draft along with either a suggested graphic or picture, or a theme or some text that could be used. Any text used in the overhead presentation could be a quote from the section that follows, a quote from another source that may be incorporated in the text, some dot points without them being a step-by-step guide to what the speaker is going to say (remember what we said about Powerpoint), or some key statistics.

The self-made speaker may well not be an expert in developing graphics. In that event, assess whether what you can provide visually will add materially to the presentation. After all, you are the visible presence and should aim to make the most of that without the inclination to feel like a second stringer just because everyone else comes along with a whiz-bang set of designs. If you feel you do need something, keep them few and keep them at a high-level overview and/or with text and graphics that convey the image of what you are saying rather than a summary of what you are saying.

3.   Take ownership of the project:

In writing for someone else, particularly a company executive or politician, the approvals and finalisation processes are where a speech is most likely to go off the rails or head in an unintended direction.

You will have structured and written the document with great care—and hopefully flair. You will have applied a stringent judgment of relevance to select the most appropriate information, statistics and case studies from the material you have been supplied or collected.

During approval and redrafting the document will cross many desks. The risk is that it becomes subject to the committee process and becomes something that resembles, to quote poet Sylvia Plath, 'a cloak of many-colored fictions'[13]. The dead hand of caution reconstructs the key points and arguments. Imaginative phrases, images and analogies are struck out or toned down to the point of blandness. I have written speeches for corporate figures that I thought would make the basis of a notable innings only to be told when I sought feedback something like, 'He got the message across without ruffling any feathers or attracting attention, and that's exactly what we wanted.' They wanted it to die, and it did. There are always these hidden agendas, and it is almost impossible for an outsider or a writer below the executive level in corporate affairs to pick up on the underlying objectives.

Some people in the organisation may see scope for a whole new approach and want it rewritten, even at this late stage.

This is also where the corporate mantras, that you have carefully avoided, are put back on the agenda. There will be business units that complain they are not getting enough of the limelight. Remember though that it should not be a sales pitch. As for the business units that might be given only a passing mention or no mention at all, it is because their stories are irrelevant in this situation. They will have their place in the sun at another time, and someone has to put that to them bluntly.

Take advice and suggestions, certainly, but be prepared to fight for every last word, sentiment and argument. Reference your statistics in case they come into question, as well as for the purpose of providing the organisation and speaker with a list of sources to substantiate, if necessary, what they are saying (as mentioned earlier, I prefer not to clutter a text with footnotes or endnotes at the stage of delivery). If somebody wants to change the emphasis of it or run their pen through parts of it, challenge them to justify their case. Rather than let them delete a section, sentence or word, challenge them to be constructive and suggest something better. Keep in mind the adage: you do not want to be told it cannot be done, but how it can be done.

Nevertheless, you need to expect there to be constant refinement and redrafting, and possibly the addition of news announcements or comments responding to current public issues, right down to the wire.

The speech, after all, is a moveable feast until it is nailed down on the last day, sometimes even in the car or on the plane to the venue. It is all part of the dynamics of the exercise and the robust relationships that surround it.

Delivering the masterpiece

TWO SCENARIOS are to be covered—one for the speaker writing their own speech, the second for the speaker who uses a speechwriter. In each situation, it is essential the speaker has a thorough comprehension of the subject and the precise wording and general flow of the text. They must also be familiar with the highlight areas of the speech, know where they are placed and virtually know them by heart. The three crucial elements are the core of the case that's being put, the basis of the point(s) being argued and the key lines that convey the message in imagery and will be remembered.

The speaker/writer does this by reading over and over the text, reading it aloud to get the right emphasis—read it to other people like friends or family, and practice in front of a mirror. It can be of considerable help in getting the emphases right to underline or run a highlighter over phrases or sentences that are intended to be given special impact, or if you prefer, to bold and italicise them in the text.

Follow these guidelines and you wll be confident in front of your audience and in accord with them.

A few cautions should be kept in mind. You will have heard first-time or occasional speakers seek your tolerance because, as they tend to say, 'I'm a bit nervous about this.' Or,

'I've never spoken in public before.' Never begin on a negative note like that. People in the audience do not want to know the torment of your soul. Should you display nervousness through the delivery, they will share your pain and embarrassment. In fact, the biggest positive you can appreciate going into it is the knowledge that they are on your side. They want to hear what you say; they genuinely want you to do well. That in itself should give you confidence. If you are a bit shaky starting off, get over the self-consciousness, focus on the people before you, feel the sense of rapport and interest that comes from the common mood of the crowd, and grow in confidence.

Throughout the preparation, get the feel of the flow, the areas of emphasis and the brief pauses where you will take a breath. Taking catch-breaths in the right places will ensure you strike the right note in the delivery, avoid the possibility of becoming racy and breathless and put you at ease in your stage presence. You could follow the example of many a good radio newsreader who in their check of the text before going on air will insert a pen-marked double slash—thus //—to indicate points within a sentence for just the slightest pause and a quick, silent breathe-in. The breaks are positioned at the right spot between two logical sequences of text. As well, a deliberate, deep-toned voice emphasis is placed on the last word or couple of words before the break and at the end of the sentence. Your voice should not fade away, nor should there be a hint of that grating Australian tonal characteristic, the rising inflexion.

Breathing correctly in the right places allows the speaker to feel more at ease and modulate their voice in line with the tone of the text. Combining that with a measured delivery that puts the emphasis where it should be also gives the speaker command of what they are saying and means the message is delivered with clarity and effect. One further point—avoid the ers and ums that people sometimes fall into as they are looking to pick up the next sentence. It will sound like you are uncertain and detract from the performance. If need be—if you are momentarily lost—just take a brief pause, which will appear more like you are doing it deliberately for effect.

A similar approach applies for the speechwriter to a government or corporate leader. They need to work with the corporate affairs or media relations chief and the senior people who have put their fingerprints on the speech and had a say in the sign-off on the final version—and, if possible, directly with the speaker—to prepare the speaker for the delivery. Again, the speaker needs to be familiar and comfortable with the text, the message, the objective in presenting it and any associated issues. Unfortunately, against the competing demands of their role at the helm of the organisation, they rarely have the time to undertake this preparatory phase with anything like thoroughness. The speechwriter or advisers close to them, therefore, need to be able to represent the engagement verbally in a single-line dot point summary—as in, here is the core message, the three things we want to get across, and the quote that will create the media headline. In the event the leader gets sidetracked between the speech briefing and their public appearance, just maybe the main points will stick.

This has to be accomplished in the broader context of the organisation's current public/market position. A speaker fronting for an organisation needs to be prepared for questioning and potential media interviews on not only their message on the day, but other issues that may be running in the public arena. In the political wing of government, for example, it so often happens a leader will deliver a major speech and face a media doorstop on the way out on a totally unrelated issue of the day. The news reports will centre on the current issue and make only passing reference, if any at all, that the political figure was speaking at the annual conference of whatever organisation it happened to be. Many a good, much laboured over speech has disappeared down the drain like that.

Most political and corporate leaders have had wide experience at public speaking and are at ease with it—in fact, in most cases revel in it. Few, though, devote the time to improve their performance or put in place a system that allows them more than peripheral input to the speech or more preparatory time. There lies a gap that many organisations could well look at filling in some way by re-examining their internal culture and processes. They should appreciate the benefit of getting the most from a public engagement and be prepared to give it a priority that ranks accordingly.

The finer points of delivery

FIRST, THERE IS THE VENUE. The speaker/writer should arrange to inspect the venue in advance and get a feel for it—where they will be sitting in the audience or on the stage during the introduction, what it is like standing behind the lectern, the configuration of the room. And test the sound system to check how the microphone picks up your voice and that your voice projects effectively.

Organisations sending speakers to an engagement should send a roadie to do a similar check and include any necessary alerts in the speaker's briefing note.

Second, the matter of attitude. Go with a respect for your audience. Your style will aim to relate to them one-to-one. Remember the radio presenter's example, except that in this case it is one person behind a lectern, under a spotlight, quite possibly terrified, but you are talking to the audience as if it was just one other person. But you are no longer squawking to your friend, 'And he/she goes ... and I couldn't believe it ...' You are the expert people have come to hear. Exert the presence that goes with it; command the attention.

Endeavour to do that from the outset. Take the lessons from speakers you have seen or heard in person, on television or radio. Watch critically how they perform, where they get it right and the audience responds warmly, and where they miss the target.

Another instructive area lies in the performances given by singers and musicians. See how they get the audience with them, the ones who want their audience to appreciate them and take away something memorable. In 2001, a favourite of mine, Billy Joel, went on a college campus tour of the US, and one performance—at the University of Philadelphia—was filmed and shown on television. It combined some of his best-known songs, snippets from others, a chat to the audience about his music, and the opportunity for students to question him. He had begun writing classical style music and had a brilliant young Japanese pianist, Richard Joo, play these pieces for him. About a third the way through the campus performance, he introduced Richard Joo. No hullo, no good evening, nice to be with you. Richard went straight to the piano and said in a finely modulated voice, 'Let's play around with time a little bit, and go back to the time of Wolfgang Amadeus Mozart. Had he written Uptown Girl, it would have sounded something like this.' And he played the first dozen or so bars of Uptown Girl à la Mozart, ending it by looking up with a wry smile. Thunderous applause filled the hall for longer than his 30-second introduction. With that simple, but creative, beginning, the audience was on his side. So it can be—even minus piano.

Your demeanour onstage will be decisive as to whether you succeed in your mission. Your attitude is to talk to one person, but there are many people. Make eye contact with them, try to develop what we might call a spatial accord. Vary the pitch

158

according to the different areas of the message—smile, laugh, niggle them to be attentive during the personal references, take absolute control when you are serious (one way: you're making the key point of the speech—put your hand palm down, slowly, deliberately, on the front of the lectern while the point sinks in).

Do not shift around too much. If you are offered the choice of a lectern with a fixed microphone or to be miked-up so you can walk around the stage, opt for the fixed setting. The mike attachment to your lapel that allows you to walk around is the kind of thing sharp salesmen do as they talk an audience into parting with their money for a worthless time-share. Speeches and presentations are also likely to be captured on camera or webcast. If you move too fast or too much, the camera will lose you. And especially don not keep shifting from one leg to the other. Again, it shows you are unsure of yourself.

Avoid the temptation to grasp the lectern with a hand on each side. You see politicians do that, as if it is a means of commanding attention—here am I, PRESENCE. In fact, it is more likely to appear to the audience or TV viewers as if they are using the lectern to hold themselves up after one too many in the members' bar.

Take care to restrict your arm movements. This is important anyway, but moreso if you are being filmed. Sudden, jerky arm movements, hands appearing at the bottom of the film screen, are distracting and add nothing to the force of the delivery. This was a habit of former Prime Minister John Howard. Seen on

TV, his arms waved around and suddenly appeared like little animations at the bottom of the screen as he became over-emphatic in pushing a point home. And thumping the lectern with your fist will only resound in the microphone or distort the sound of your voice.

The way to do it is periodically raise your arm to add some urgency to the point you are making. As you are moving through a passage designed to get the audience onside or convince them of your case, extend a rounded arm as a gesture that embraces them. This gentle, warm approach is more inclusive in bringing you and the audience together.

In short, use the range of techniques described here to project yourself as well as your message. The two have an integral fit. Your endeavour should be to create a feeling of warmth, of interest, even excitement, around the images, ideas and arguments you are putting forward. This way, your audience will go away with the clear impression you have endowed them with something good or worthwhile or different; you have been a person of distinction, like a friend who has risen to a great occasion. As importantly, you will carry the satisfaction of knowing you have done it in style.

11. People, take note!

More than a one-night stand

The age of information and communications and the increasing complexity of the communication role mean the speech is rarely a stand-alone event. It has far greater potential, and practical application in fact, than to serve as a one-night stand or fade into a haze of cheap chardonnay or shiraz over lunch.

The speech has an important role in capturing the attention of your immediate and broader constituencies and getting your message across to them, keeping them in the picture, convincing the sceptics, in positioning the organisation and the speaker publicly and securing positive media coverage.

That goes for Telstra (read the headlines since the change in management to see how a household brand has been tarnished) and BHP Billiton and equally for an individual to whom public profile may be of advantage for any one of a number of reasons. For example, getting known serves as an avenue for business promotion for someone like me who operates as a solo free agent (although, confession time: after running a seminar for a large corporate, about a third of the audience were of a consensus that I was probably a better writer than presenter—but there were others who loved it!). Getting your name top of mind, even up to afterthought level, in the market can be tough for free agents who work mainly out of home with a cat for company and for small and new enterprises as they sweat on jobs and cash flow in those early years. A positive profile can be beneficial, too, for career development—make a name for yourself and await the stampede of people handing out job assignments. And it is a pathway for people aiming to go into public life in some form.

In the case of both the organisational leader and the individual, an impressive performance before an influential audience places them in demand as a speaker, which is good for both. By standing out in a delivery, Organisation Man/Woman (again, you will not get me into the correctness of saying person— I would go for humanoid or homo sapiens first) projects a positive image of their organisation and of themselves as leaders. This is the pathway to being in demand as a speaker at conferences run by business groups and national and international business sector and government conferences, to get a seat on centre stage. The building of respect that attaches to that is invaluable for an organisation, and organisations should more actively seek out those opportunities for their key people—except, that is, if they happened at the time to be high on the rung at HIH, Enron or WorldCom or have a name like Alan Bond, but they already knew that.

In large, diverse and widely spread organisations, statements by their leaders are also an invaluable source of internal information—a means of keeping your own people informed.

Establishing a name as a speaker also opens ongoing opportunities for individuals to get on the speaker circuit. They may not have a corporation or government behind them but possibly represent a non-government group or present a public point of view, or have been there, done that and happen to be a swimmer with a name like, and the looks of, Jodie Henry, or who have a few damn good ideas and a good way of presenting them, or are just good old-fashioned entertainers with a new twist. There are so many functions being held, covering so many fields, that a lot of people who can hold the floor are turning to the professional speaker circuit and doing nicely from it. The beauty of that is you do not have to write a totally new speech each time. An adaptation of the standing A1-Draft 14 will fit the bill.

There is good money to be made out of it—probably not as much as writing a speech under contract, but the circuit is more regular and reliable and there are promoters in the field that have large stables of public speakers. Jodie Henry is one who will have it made if she wants. People would pay money, too, to hear how Alan Bond continues to live a better lifestyle than 90 per cent of the rest of us, and how he made it there (several times over) in the first place. Martha Stewart, the household diva as she has been called, announced the intention to produce a book from her time in prison for fraud in 2004. The figure talked around at the time it was revealed was in the order of US$5 million. Then, her time done, there is the speaking circuit, magazine articles and talk show appearances. A whole new and very profitable life for a woman who did her time in a prison that was established for what they nicely called 'fallen' women.

Doing time—without going to jail

NOTORIETY MIGHT BE MORE ALLURING, but I would suggest doing the time as a speaker representing a respectable organisation or on your own account as the best and most certain way to accumulate credits.

But speeches can get lost in the absence of a plan to push them for all they are worth. Every speech of note should be accompanied by a tailored promotional strategy built around the relevant interest groups and interested individuals. Calculate this centred on your own interest in terms of who you want to be aware of it.

The major speeches should be posted on your organisation's Internet site and Intranet and be widely circulated internally. They can, and should, be webcast live and for archiving. If appropriate, the webcast and online text can be linked to other relevant sites. People likely to have a particular interest can be advised in a teaser summary in your next newsletter, which these days will naturally be a graphic email production ... Right?

If it is a media event, obviously the reporters covering it will want full texts. You just need to add a caution at the top—the words, Check Against Delivery—in case there are departures from the text. An advance media strategy is essential for a keynote address for which you want to get the widest possible coverage.

The most effective way to achieve this is to send the newspaper editors and their features' editors an embargoed copy the day before delivery, and put in a call to let them know it is coming and it has oomph. With a big, big speech, it is possible to get a double coverage by allowing the papers to run an article on the morning it is to be delivered saying the minister/chief executive/whoever will today announce ... A preview appears, and the speech will then be covered extensively on radio and TV on the day, and the detail from the delivery will appear on TV that night and in the newspapers the next morning. This is the saturation principle. Giving the editors and heads of features a text in advance also opens the possibility of getting a summary of the speech printed at some length on the Op-Ed (opposite editorial, for the uninitiated) page of the papers. We did this very effectively with many of Jeff Kennett's keynote speeches. There are also situations in which you may be aware a single newspaper or journalist has a particular interest in the issues you will be talking about, and you may elect to give them an exclusive on the advance release. Beware, though, that by doing that you might burn your bridges with the rest of the media for the future. But if you have the status, they will come back. Assess the situation carefully. If it warrants, take a who-cares line. We'll burn that bridge when we come to it!

Following this through, it also pays to send advance copies to producers of the main radio talk station producers and phone them in advance to assess their interest. As well as gaining all the newspaper and radio and TV news coverage, you can spend the day on radio doing extended interviews that allow you to expound the main themes of the speech over and over—and get feedback via talkback (the people on mobiles who ask the inane questions, but they will also get the message this way and give you an idea of how it is going down).

It is a good idea to have a stack of copies of the text at the venue to provide to the host organisation, the organisations represented in the audience and anyone who wants to pick up a copy on the way out.

Having a take-away copy to read cements the message in their minds. The spoken word tends to disappear into the ether immediately it is been uttered. The audience, by the time they have finished applauding, will remember at best some of the key points, maybe a catchy phrase or two, a particular statistic and perhaps a case study or anecdotal reference that is pertinent to them. But no more. A good test of this theory, if you need convincing, is to listen to a radio news bulletin with someone else. When it ends, ask them without prior warning to list the first three headlines in order. Nine out of 10 will fail the test.

Where appropriate, the speech should also be circulated to other organisations and people. These could include governments and key figures within government, government departments and agencies, business associations, advocacy and watchdog groups, and any public organisations assessed as having an interest.

The aim, quite achievable with these strategies, is to get yourself more than the statutory five minutes of fame that is due to everyone.

12. Evaluation

Once the applause dies down, it is time to begin learning the lessons for next time. And the applause itself is the first sign to note, followed by the initial comments of people around you.

If you, as the writer, were there, make a critical assessment of how it went—how the speaker handled the text, whether it came across clearly, how the audience received it, the level of interest shown in question time if there was one, the tone of the questions they asked. And see how the media treats it—whether they picked up the core message and used the key quotes you tailored to them, whether they took some obscure angle and went off on a tangent or used it as the basis for criticism. Did they concentrate on the speech, or overlook it and focus on a negative line of questioning? Or did they doorstop the speaker on an entirely different issue, and cover that in their stories and not even refer to the speech? What was the extent of media coverage over the following 24 hours? What was the level and nature of the follow up? Was it a raging topic on talkback radio the next day? Were there people, with either supportive or contrary views, who felt compelled to comment publicly? Is there a sense it has been good for the business? Has the relevant government minister been on the phone to invite the speaker in for coffee?

Combine this with feedback from your colleagues who were there and people in the office who have read it subsequently. Assess whether the general view is that it did in fact make a positive contribution to the organisation's business and communication objectives.

See if you can also, either face-to-face or indirectly, get the speaker's impression.

Over the following days, talk to the host organisation to get its reaction and the nature of any responses it may have received. A good sign would be if they want your speaker back for their major event next year.

Writer/speakers should make a similar evaluation.

By listing all these things in a table and making qualitative assessments on even a rudimentary positive/negative scale, you end up with a general idea of whether it hit the mark and the areas where it may have gone amiss.

A speech written for someone else is difficult to get right. There is a chance the delivery may have made it sound quite different to your perception as to the way it would go from the final text that was signed off. The individual writer/speaker faces a more subjective challenge in preparing a speech, which may leave lingering doubts up to the last moment. But as has been asserted throughout this work, a comprehensive, carefully planned, logical approach, some creative flair thrown in, and thorough preparation for the delivery will engender the confidence you need to pass the ultimate test. In fact, just having done it is a confidence builder in itself.

Assessment and feedback will pinpoint the successful elements and troublespots and allow you to look at it in a positive way as a valuable lesson and as reassurance for next time.

I have a saying relating to speechwriters that while you might live by the pen, you still die by the sword. But take heart that they do not always shoot the messenger. If you have been meticulous in your approach, if you have put your heart into it and done it as well as you can, it will have worked and there will come another day.

Endnotes

1. Safire, William, 1992, *Lend Me Your Ears: Great Speeches in History*, W.W. Norton & Company

2. Watson, Don, 2003, *Recollections of a Bleeding Heart: Portrait of Paul Keating PM*, Random House Australia

3. Reston, James, 'Repairing the ship of state', article published 23 January 1970, The New York Times

4. LaBarre, Polly, 2004, 'Do you have the will to lead?' Gruner & Jahr USA Publishing, first published February 2000 in Fast Company Magazine, based on an audio-cassette by Peter Koestenbaum, 'Do you have the will to lead?: real world philosophy for leaders'

5. Byrne, David, 'Learning to Love PowerPoint', originally published September 2003 in Wired Magazine

6. Tufte, Edward R., 2003, *The Cognitive Style of PowerPoint*, Graphics Press, Cheshire, CT, USA

7. Pink, Daniel H. 2001, *Free Agent Nation*, Warner Books, Inc., New York

8. Pink, Daniel H. 2005, *A Whole New Mind*, first published by arrangement with Riverhead Books, a member of Penguin Group (USA) Inc., published in Australia and New Zealand by Allen & Unwin, Sydney

9. Ibid, pp 100—101

10. Ibid, p 107

11. McKee, Robert 1999, *Story: Substance, Structure, Style, and the Principles of Screenwriting*, Methuen Publishing Limited, London; and refer to his web site: www.mckeestory.com

12. Lederer, William J. and Burdick, Eugene, *The Ugly American*, W.W. Norton & Company, first published 1958, a longtime bestseller for its exposé of American arrogance, incompetence, and corruption in South-East Asia and how the US was losing the struggle with Communism in Asia

13. Plath, Sylvia 1981, 'Tale of a Tub', published in *Collected Poems*, a collection of her work post-1956, Harper & Row, New York

Project Q

Q—www.q2write.com—is an international community of writers of all kinds, of publishers, readers ... anyone with a passion for the written word. Author Kevin Balshaw manages the site. Q is a publishing outlet for writers with drawers full of rejection slips, a source of encouragement for anyone who believes they have a book or a story in them but have never got around to it.

Q2write provides MSS assessment, editing, proofing, design and publishing services for writers—from ISBN numbers to file preparation and upload for print-on-demand publication or submission to a publisher.

It contains, or links to, all the practical information required to produce a professional written work and get it published—as a family memoir, or for a worldwide market.

It is a place where people can record their thoughts or insights or sound off about things, mount campaigns on local issues or join national and worldwide campaigns ... with like-minded people who give a damn.

Think of *qi*, the inspirational life force that is the basis of much of Chinese philosophy and medicine, and there you have it.

Made in the USA
Lexington, KY
12 March 2010